Curriculum Visions

Spelling

Teacher's Resource Book 5

Sarah Lindsay

Curriculum Visions

Spelling

First published in 2006 by
Atlantic Europe Publishing Company Ltd

Text copyright © Sarah Lindsay 2006

The right of Sarah Lindsay to be identified as
the author of this work has been asserted by her
in accordance with the Copyright, Designs and
Patents Act 1988.

Illustrations and design copyright © 2006
Atlantic Europe Publishing Company Ltd

Curriculum Visions Spelling
Teacher's Resource Book 5
A CIP record for this book is available
from the British Library.

ISBN-10: 1-86214-520-2
ISBN-13: 978-1-86214-520-7

**This product is manufactured from sustainable
managed forests. For every tree cut down at least
one more is planted.**

Author
Sarah Lindsay

Art Director
Duncan McCrae

Senior Designer
Adele Humphries

Editors
Robert Anderson and Gillian Gatehouse

Illustrations
Dave Woodroffe
Mark Stacey (cover and pages 2, 5, 6)

Designed and produced by
EARTHSCAPE EDITIONS

Printed in China by
WKT Company Ltd

Contents

An Introduction to *Curriculum Visions Spelling*

Why should we teach spelling?

Effective spelling is central to a child's self-confidence. Being able to spell competently means confident writing. This is a motivating factor in the learning and enjoyment of all writing tasks across the curriculum, and in having the confidence to become better spellers. So, teaching the basic foundations for good spelling can trigger a virtuous cycle.

Spelling competence is also perceived within society as indicative of a level of literacy, educational attainment and intellect. Critically, a competent speller is less likely to be judged negatively in these respects as he or she moves through their schooling and eventually into further education and employment.

Despite this, national test results continue to suggest that overall there is still an inadequate knowledge among some pupils of spelling rules and conventions. However, an organised and systematic approach to the teaching of spelling, as contained within the heart of the National Literacy Strategy, has been shown to raise levels of achievement significantly in those schools making a real commitment to the improvement of spelling.

The NLS

The NLS Framework for Teaching posits that pupils become successful readers by learning to use a range of strategies to get to the meaning of a text: phonic; grammatical knowledge; word recognition and graphic knowledge; context cues. It states that although teachers know about these strategies they are often 'over cautious about the teaching of phonics – sound and spelling'. It says that:

It is vital that pupils are taught to use these word level strategies effectively. Research evidence shows that pupils do not learn to distinguish between the different sounds of words simply by being exposed to books.

They need to be taught to do this. When they begin to read, most pupils tend to see words as images with a particular shape and pattern. They tend not to understand that words are made up of letters used in particular combinations that correspond with spoken sounds. It is essential that pupils are taught these basic decoding and spelling skills from the outset.

(NLS Framework for Teaching, page 4)

Curriculum Visions Spelling – An effective word level strategy

The Framework makes it clear that there should be a 'strong and systematic emphasis' on the teaching of spelling. So how does *Curriculum Visions Spelling* support the objectives of the Framework? The word level skill objectives in the NLS Framework include:

▶ the ability to discriminate between the separate sounds in words;

▶ the learning of the letters and letter combinations most commonly used to spell these sounds;

▶ the ability to write words by combining the spelling patterns of their sounds.

Curriculum Visions Spelling is absolutely focused on meeting these objectives, and does so in a clear, easy-to-follow and systematic fashion. It maps closely to the spelling and vocabulary objectives of the word level strand in the Framework at Key Stages 1 and 2 and helps you, the teacher, achieve both balance and coverage of the spelling-related objectives specified for each term.

Curriculum Visions Spelling also complements programmes based on synthetic phonics.

Word Level
Reception year   • Phonological awareness, phonics and spelling   • Word recognition, graphic knowledge and spelling   • Vocabulary extension
Key Stage 1   • Phonological awareness, phonics and spelling   • Word recognition, graphic knowledge and spelling   • Vocabulary extension
Key Stage 2   • Revision and consolidation from Key Stage 1 (to the end of Y3)   • Spelling strategies   • Spelling conventions and rules   • Vocabulary extension

How does *Curriculum Visions Spelling* deliver an effective spelling programme?

Curriculum Visions Spelling is designed to be easy for you to use by being structured in a way that children will find accessible, with clear targets and differentiated tasks.

The instructional language is clear, direct and carefully tailored to the needs of pupils at each level and age group. The activities are gently differentiated in difficulty and will help build pupils' confidence and reinforce their spelling knowledge, skills and competence.

We have thought long and hard about the layout and content of each unit. Our intention has been to provide you, the teacher, with a progressive and useful scheme for delivering the word level work in the NLS. The scheme has also been structured and devised to accommodate the requirements of teachers delivering the curricula of Scotland, Wales and Northern Ireland.

The main features of both the *Pupil Book* and *Teacher's Resource Book* are shown below.

Pupil Book

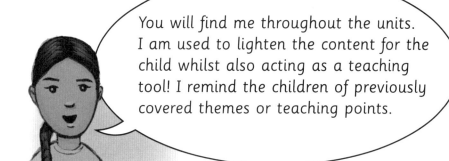

You will find me throughout the units. I am used to lighten the content for the child whilst also acting as a teaching tool! I remind the children of previously covered themes or teaching points.

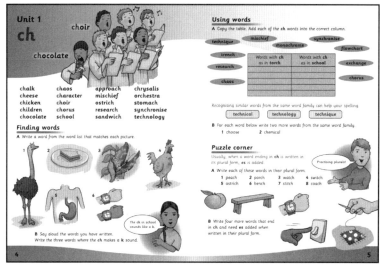

Spelling focus

Each unit has a particular spelling as its main focus. The labelled picture helps the child recognise the focus of the unit immediately.

Word list

There follows four columns of words that relate to the *Spelling focus* of the unit. The *Word list* is intended as an aid to children working through the unit, particularly in the *Finding words* section. These words, where possible, increase in difficulty. They can be found listed in the *Look Cover Say Write Check* photocopiable tables (pages 87–93 of this book), ideal to be used as daily/weekly spellings. You, as the teacher, will need to decide which child should receive which spelling lists – one particular child might be given the first column to learn whilst the next child is challenged with the first three columns to learn.

Finding words

This is a gentle introduction to the words within the unit *Spelling focus*. It encourages the children to make words with related spellings.

Using words

This section extends the child's knowledge of the *Spelling focus*. He or she will have to search beyond the words found in the *Word list* for answers.

Puzzle corner

The *Puzzle corner* is a more light-hearted exercise that often focuses on vocabulary work. Where possible it is linked to the *Spelling focus* of the unit.

Teacher's Resource Book

Targets

These are the targets specifically covered in this unit, both in the *Spelling focus* and the *Puzzle corner* exercise.

Word list

A quick reference for the teacher. It is particularly useful when planning either different group work or spelling homework for individual children.

Some other relevant words

This list covers further words using the spelling patterns found in the *Word list*. In addition, other words are provided that might be useful for extension work or classroom discussions.

Relevant high/medium-frequency words

High or medium-frequency words that can be linked to the spelling focus of the unit.

Copymaster/ Homework answers

These are the answers to the photocopiable pages that link with the *Spelling focus* (Copymaster A) and the activity encompassed within the *Puzzle corner* (Copymaster B) of each unit. The work covered in the unit is reinforced and sometimes taken on a step further. Both activity sheets are ideal as homework or as further work in the classroom.

Suggestions

A few extension activities have been suggested and/or background information provided.

Pupil Book answers

These are the answers to the *Pupil Book* material.

Assessments

There are two assessments found on pages 82–83 and 84–85, each one covering either the first 11 units or the second 11 units. Notes and Answers to the Assessments can be found on page 81.

Word lists

The *Word lists* (copies of the *Word list* found in each unit) on pages 88–93 are designed to be photocopied and used as the spelling homework for the week. If required they can be used in conjunction with the *Look Cover Say Write Check* table found on page 96. The words can be split according to the ability of the child.

There are then further *Word lists* on pages 94–95 that cover (in groups of six words) the medium-frequency words with which the children should become familiar as quickly as possible.

Scheme summary

		Book 1		Book 2		Book 3
Unit 1	a	alphabetical order	ea ee	plurals (+s)	a–e ai ay	verb + ing
Unit 2	e	equipment labels	ay a–e ai	vowel / consonant	ee ea	syllables
Unit 3	i	high-frequency words	y i–e igh	common irregular words	ie i–e y igh	misspelt words
Unit 4	o	common spelling patterns	o–e oa ow	past tense (+ed)	o–e oa ow	categorising words
Unit 5	u	alphabetical order	ew ue u–e oo	high-frequency words	oo ew u–e ue	inferring meaning
Unit 6	sh	words within words	ck	present tense (+ing)	le	synonyms
Unit 7	ch	colour words	u oo	collections of words	un dis	thesaurus work
Unit 8	th	topic words	ar	antonyms	air are ear ere	dictionary work
Unit 9	ll	high-frequency words	oy oi	high-frequency words	or ore aw au	root words
Unit 10	ss ff	classroom captions	ow ou	syllables	er ir ur	dialogue words
Unit 11	ng	days of the week	tch nch	same sound, different spelling pattern	de re pre	opposites
Unit 12	cl fl sl	words within words	air	un prefix	+ y	compound words
Unit 13	dr gr tr	plurals (+s)	are ear	compound words	+ er + est	singular and plural
Unit 14	nd	word collections	or ore	dis prefix	n't	definitions
Unit 15	st sp	high-frequency words	aw au	syllables	silent k and w	verb + ing
Unit 16	str	ed endings	er	synonyms	+ ly	alphabetical order (second place)
Unit 17	nk	vowel letters	ir	same spelling pattern, different sound	+ ful + less	inferring meaning
Unit 18	ee	months of the year	ur	common irregular words	plurals	homonyms
Unit 19	ai	common spelling patterns	wh ph ch	ful suffix	mis	short words in longer words
Unit 20	ie i–e	consonant letters	wa	high-frequency words	qu	expressions
Unit 21	oa	ing endings	ear	ly suffix	apostrophe	synonyms
Unit 22	oo	numbers to twenty	ea	shades of meaning	non ex anti	dictionary work

	Book 4		Book 5		Book 6	
Unit 1	less ness	misspelt words	ch	plurals (es)	soft c and g	connectives
Unit 2	er	homophones	ent ence	misspelt words	silent letters	misspelt words
Unit 3	al	definitions	ant ance	expressions	able ible	unstressed vowels
Unit 4	ment	high-frequency words	auto bi	words ending in a, i, o and u	aero auto aqua	spelling similar words
Unit 5	verb + s ed ing	irregular tense changes	ly	plurals (ies)	bi con co	words changing over time
Unit 6	hood ship	alphabetical order (third place)	tele trans circum	synonyms	graph scope	origins of proper names
Unit 7	on en	making verbs	words to watch	plurals (ves)	cc	new words
Unit 8	double letters	changing vocabulary	silent letters b g c	onomatopoeia	tele tri oct	etymological dictionary
Unit 9	ic	alternative words	ful	double consonants (+ ed + ing)	dge age	mnemonics
Unit 10	un re non dis	gender words	letter strings	technical words	gue	unstressed vowels
Unit 11	words ending in f	definitions	soft c	antonyms	ex sub	word origins
Unit 12	ight	alphabetical order (fourth place)	soft g	homophones	ic	proverbs
Unit 13	ory ery ary	making adjectives	ure	possessive pronouns	ous	words changing over time
Unit 14	ough	medium-frequency words	al	expressions	inter micro	argument words
Unit 15	able	compound words	el	acronyms	dd	spelling rules
Unit 16	ible	diminutives	un im il	omission of letters	ist ian	mnemonics
Unit 17	ive	prefixes	er est ish	personally written definitions	or ar	misspelt words
Unit 18	ie ei	misspelt words	ion	thesaurus work	ary ery ory	dictionary work
Unit 19	tion	its and it's	en ify ise	modifying e	words to watch	spelling rules
Unit 20	sion	homophones	tt	changing tenses	nn	similes and metaphors
Unit 21	wa	suffixes	aw au	unstressed vowels	ise	word games
Unit 22	ss	root words	ph	dialect variations	ive	inventing words

Book 5 targets

Unit page	Spelling focus	Targets	Puzzle corner	Targets
Unit 1	ch	• to use independent spelling strategies, including building up spellings by syllabic parts, using known prefixes, suffixes and common letter strings and using visual skills	plurals (es)	• to investigate, collect and classify spelling patterns in pluralisation (+s, +es), construct rules for regular spellings
Unit 2	ent ence	• to use independent spelling strategies, including building up spellings by syllabic parts, using known prefixes, suffixes and common letter strings; building words from other known words and from awareness of the meaning or derivations of words; using visual skills	misspelt words	• to identify misspelt words in own writing; to keep individual lists; to learn to spell them
Unit 3	ant ance	• to use independent spelling strategies, including building up spellings by syllabic parts, using known prefixes, suffixes and common letter strings; building words from other known words and from awareness of the meaning or derivations of words; using visual skills	expressions	• to collect and classify a range of idiomatic phrases, clichés and expressions. Compare, discuss, speculate about meanings/origins and check in dictionaries; use in own writing and be aware of when it is appropriate to use these in writing
Unit 4	auto bi	• to collect and investigate the meanings and spellings of words using the prefixes *auto* and *bi* • to identify word roots in order to extend vocabulary and provide support for spelling	words ending in a, i, o and u	• to examine the properties of words ending in vowels other than the letter *e* • to identify everyday words which have been borrowed from other languages, and to understand how this might give clues to spelling
Unit 5	ly	• to use adverbs to qualify verbs in writing dialogue	plurals (ies)	• to investigate, collect and classify spelling patterns in pluralisation (+ies), construct rules for regular spellings
Unit 6	tele trans circum	• to collect and investigate the meanings and spellings of words using the prefixes *tele*, *trans* and *circum*	synonyms	• to explain the differences between synonyms; collect, classify and order sets of words to identify shades of meaning
Unit 7	words to watch	• to use independent spelling strategies, including: building words from other known words and from awareness of the meaning or derivations of words; using visual skills	plurals (ves)	• to investigate, collect and classify spelling patterns in pluralisation (+ves), construct rules for regular spellings

Unit page	Spelling focus	Targets	Puzzle corner	Targets
Unit 8	silent letters b g c	• to use independent spelling strategies including: applying knowledge of spelling rules and exceptions; using visual skills	onomatopoeia	• to explore onomatopoeia: collect, invent and use words whose meaning is represented in their sounds
Unit 9	ful	• to explore spelling patterns of consonants and formulate rules: *ll* in 'full' becomes *l* when used as a suffix	double consonants (+ ed + ing)	• to explore spelling patterns of consonants and formulate rules: words ending with a single consonant preceded by a short vowel double the consonant before adding *ing* etc.
Unit 10	letter strings	• to investigate words which have common letter strings but different pronunciations	technical words	• to search for, collect, define and spell technical words derived from work in other subjects
Unit 11	soft c	• to explore spelling patterns of consonants and formulate rules: *c* is usually soft when followed by *i* • to recognise and spell the suffix *cian*	antonyms	• to investigate further antonyms
Unit 12	soft g	• to explore spelling patterns of consonants and formulate rules	homophones	• to distinguish between homophones, i.e. words with common pronunciations but different spellings
Unit 13	ure	• to use independent spelling strategies, including building up spellings by syllabic parts, using known suffixes and common letter strings; building words from other known words and from awareness of the meaning or derivations of words; using visual skills • to identify word roots in order to extend vocabulary and provide support for spelling	possessive pronouns	• the correct use and spelling of possessive pronouns, linked to work on grammar, e.g. their, theirs; your, yours; my, mine
Unit 14	al	• to use independent spelling strategies, including building up spellings by syllabic parts, using known prefixes, suffixes and common letter strings; building words from other known words and from awareness of the meaning or derivations of words; using visual skills	expressions	• to investigate metaphorical expressions and figures of speech from everyday life
Unit 15	el	• to use independent spelling strategies, including building up spellings by syllabic parts, using known suffixes and common letter strings; building words from other known words and from awareness of the meaning or derivations of words; using visual skills	acronyms	• to understand how words can be formed from longer words, through the use of acronyms

Unit page	Spelling focus	Targets	Puzzle corner	Targets
Unit 16	un im il	• to transform words, e.g. negation	omission of letters	• to understand how words can be formed from longer words, e.g. through the omission of letters
Unit 17	er est ish	• to transform words, e.g. making comparatives	personally written definitions	• to compile personally written definitions, e.g. of slang, technical terms
Unit 18	ion	• to transform words, e.g. verbs to nouns	thesaurus work	• to use a thesaurus and understand its purpose
Unit 19	en ify ise	• to transform words, e.g. nouns (and adjectives) to verbs	modifying e	• to investigate and learn spelling rules: words ending in modifying e, drop e when adding ing
Unit 20	tt	• to use independent spelling strategies, including: building up spellings by syllabic parts, using common letter strings; applying knowledge of spelling rules and exceptions; using visual skills	changing tenses	• to explore spelling patterns of consonants and formulate rules: words ending with a single consonant preceded by a short vowel double the consonant before adding ing etc. • to transform words, e.g. changing tenses
Unit 21	aw au	• to use independent spelling strategies, including building up spellings by syllabic parts, using known prefixes, suffixes and common letter strings; building words from other known words and from awareness of the meaning or derivations of words; using visual skills	unstressed vowels	• to spell unstressed vowels in polysyllabic words • to use dictionaries efficiently to explore spellings, meanings
Unit 22	ph	• to use independent spelling strategies, including building up spellings by syllabic parts, using known prefixes, suffixes and common letter strings; building words from other known words and from awareness of the meaning or derivations of words; using visual skills	dialect variations	• to understand how words vary across dialects

Spelling Book 5 • Book 5 targets • © *Sarah Lindsay/Atlantic Europe Publishing 2006*

Unit notes, answers and copymasters
Units 1–22

Unit 1
ch

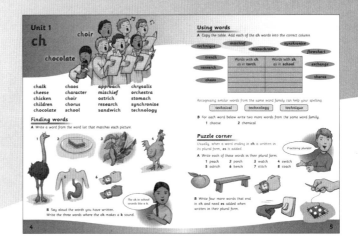

Targets

- to use independent spelling strategies, including building up spellings by syllabic parts, using known prefixes, suffixes and common letter strings and using visual skills

- to investigate, collect and classify spelling patterns in pluralisation (+s, +es), construct rules for regular spellings

Word list

chalk	chaos	approach	chrysalis
cheese	character	mischief	orchestra
chicken	choir	ostrich	stomach
children	chorus	research	synchronise
chocolate	school	sandwich	technology

Some other relevant words

chair choose choosy chose chosen dispatch
exchange flowchart match

chemistry chlorinate chord monochrome

Relevant high/medium-frequency words

much school

change children watch

Pupil Book answers

Finding words

A **1** ostrich **2** sandwich **3** chrysalis **4** chicken
5 stomach **6** synchronise

B chrysalis stomach synchronise

Using words

A

Words with **ch** as in **torch**	Words with **ch** as in **school**
trench	technique
exchange	chaos
research	monochrome
flowchart	synchronise
mischief	chorus

B e.g. **1** chose, choice **2** chemistry, chemist

Puzzle corner

A **1** peaches **2** porches **3** watches **4** switches
5 ostriches **6** benches **7** stitches **8** coaches

B Four more words that end in **ch** and need **es** added when written in their plural form.

Copymaster/Homework answers

Unit 1A

A **1** technology **2** handkerchief **3** exchange
4 orchestra **5** chair **6** chocolate

B Table completed correctly with **ch** words.

Unit 1B

1 boxes **2** bushes **3** matches **4** pigs or piglets
5 classes **6** foxes **7** plates or dishes **8** pictures
9 addresses

Suggestions

- Explain to the children that *ch* is a common letter string. Highlight the fact that although words may have the same letter strings it doesn't necessarily mean the pronunciation of the letter string will be the same.

- Usually, if a word with *ch* comes from the Greek language, the *ch* sounds *k*, e.g. chemistry.

- Plurals have previously been covered in Book 1, Unit 13; Book 2, Unit 1 and Book 3, Unit 13 and are further covered in this book in Units 5 and 7.

- Build a class dictionary of plurals. Each child could be responsible for a page which would illustrate a plural, its singular form, a definition and a picture.

Name: _____ Date: _____

A Use the clues to find the correct **ch** word.

exchange	orchestra	chocolate
chair	technology	handkerchief

1 A subject you learn in school. _____

2 Used with a runny nose. _____

3 To swap. _____

4 A group of musicians. _____

5 Something you sit on. _____

6 Tasty and sweet. _____

B Complete this table with **ch** words.

ch as in match	**ch** as in choir

Name: _____   Date: _____

Remember...
when we write most words in
their plural form we just add **s**
BUT
if a word ends in **s**, **x**, **sh** or **ch**
we usually add **es**.

Unit 1B

Plurals

Write a label for each of the pictures.

1

_____

2

_____

3

_____

4

_____

5

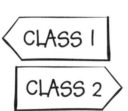

CLASS 1

CLASS 2

_____

6

_____

7

_____

8

_____

9

25 Spelling Road
Book Village
BV10 3AB

12 The Street
Wordtown
WT3 1XY

_____

   Spelling Book 5 • Unit 1B • plurals (es) • © *Sarah Lindsay/Atlantic Europe Publishing 2006*

Unit 2
ent
ence

Targets

- to use independent spelling strategies, including building up spellings by syllabic parts, using known prefixes, suffixes and common letter strings; building words from other known words and from awareness of the meaning or derivations of words; using visual skills

- to identify misspelt words in own writing; to keep individual lists; to learn to spell them

Word list

agent	fence	different	experience
event	pence	excellent	licence
invent	science	frequent	presence
moment	sentence	obedient	reference
present	silence	transparent	sequence

Some other relevant words

absent accent advent cement client competent consistent content convent current deficient dependent efficient equivalent evident extent fluent imminent independent intent lenient magnificent parent patient permanent president pungent recent reminiscent repellent rodent scent sent sentiment silent spent succulent talent tent urgent vent went

absence competence consequence consistence correspondence defence difference essence evidence excellence existence obedience occurrence offence preference recurrence residence subsequence

Relevant high/medium-frequency words

different (+ suffix)

Pupil Book answers

Finding words

A **1** agent **2** obedient **3** present **4** sequence or sentence **5** fence **6** frequent

B A sentence/sentences describing the picture at the beginning of the unit, including as many **ent** and **ence** words as possible.

Using words

A

	+ent	+ence
differ	different	difference
sil	silent	silence
intellig	intelligent	intelligence
evid	evident	evidence

obedi	obedient	obedience
innoc	innocent	innocence
consequ	consequent	consequence

B Two sentences, each with a pair of words written in the table above.

Puzzle corner

David was bored. It was <u>pouring</u> with rain <u>outside</u> and the wind was gusting. <u>Suddenly</u>, <u>there</u> was a huge crash and he dived for cover under the table. <u>Eventually</u>, when he felt a little braver he <u>peered</u> over the table to <u>discover</u> he was now <u>sitting</u> in the middle of a tree! A <u>squirrel</u>, looking as <u>stunned</u> as David, looked at him for a <u>second</u> and then ran <u>off</u> <u>through</u> the <u>branches</u>. David could <u>hear</u> his mother calling… Maybe the day wasn't going to be <u>boring</u> <u>after</u> all!

Copymaster/Homework answers

Unit 2A

A **1** succulent **2** existence **3** magnificent **4** urgent **5** preference

B Two sentences, each with an **ent** or **ence** word of the child's choice.

Unit 2B

A The following words circled: **1** sometime **2** brother **3** swimming **4** around **5** children **6** opened

B **1** together **2** receive **3** different **4** stopped **5** experience

Suggestions

- Write some words covered in this unit on cards and their definitions on other cards. Ask the children to match the definitions with the correct *ent* or *ence* words.

- There are a few verbs that end with *ent*, e.g. cement, invent, prevent, resent, relent, present, frequent.

- Further extension work can be done highlighting the fact that many adjectives ending in *ent* have related nouns that end in *ency*, e.g. urgent – urgency (decent, frequent, lenient, transparent, etc.).

- Misspelt words have previously been covered in Book 3, Unit 3 and Book 4, Units 1 and 18.

- Ask the children to make up mnemonics of words they frequently misspell.

Unit 2A

A Match each of the **ent** or **ence** words in the box with its synonyms.

Remember, a **synonym** is a word with the same or very similar meaning to another word!

existence	urgent
magnificent	succulent
preference	

1 juicy   moist _____

2 survival   being _____

3 wonderful   brilliant _____

4 vital   pressing _____

5 favourite   liking _____

B Write two sentences, each with an **ent** or **ence** word.

1 _____

_____

2 _____

_____

Name: _____   Date: _____

Unit 2B

A Spot the correct spelling!
Circle the word that is spelt correctly.

If you are stuck
on a word check
it in a dictionary!

1	sometim	sometime	sumetime
2	brother	bruther	brothur
3	swiming	swimming	swimmig
4	around	arond	arownd
5	children	chidren	childrn
6	openned	opennd	opened

B Each of these words is misspelt.
Spell each word correctly.

1 togther   _____

2 recieve   _____

3 diffrent   _____

4 stoped   _____

5 experiance   _____

Unit 3
ant
ance

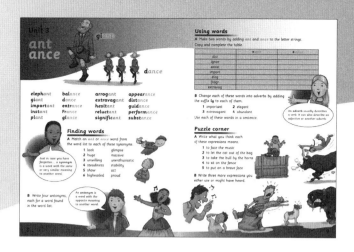

Targets

- to use independent spelling strategies, including building up spellings by syllabic parts, using known prefixes, suffixes and common letter strings; building words from other known words and from awareness of the meaning or derivations of words; using visual skills

- to collect and classify a range of idiomatic phrases, clichés and expressions. Compare, discuss, speculate about meanings/origins and check in dictionaries; use in own writing and be aware of when it is appropriate to use these in writing

Word list

elephant	balance	arrogant	appearance
giant	dance	extravagant	distance
important	entrance	hesitant	guidance
instant	France	reluctant	performance
plant	glance	significant	substance

Some other relevant words

abundant adamant attendant blatant buoyant constant currant dependant distant dominant elegant emigrant extravagant exuberant flippant fragrant gallant irrelevant jubilant peasant pendant pheasant pleasant pregnant redundant relevant restaurant slant stagnant transplant truant valiant vibrant

abundance advance alliance arrogance attendance chance defiance disturbance dominance elegance extravagance instance insurance irrelevance maintenance nuisance prance reassurance reluctance remembrance resistance romance stance trance

Relevant high/medium-frequency words

important (+ suffix)

Pupil Book answers

Finding words

A 1 glance 2 giant 3 reluctant 4 balance
  5 performance 6 arrogant

B e.g. giant – miniature   entrance – exit   glance – stare
  important – trivial

Using words

A

	+ant	+ance
dist	distant	distance
ignor	ignorant	ignorance

assist	assistant	assistance
import	important	importance
eleg	elegant	elegance
fragr	fragrant	fragrance
extravag	extravagant	extravagance

B 1 importantly 2 elegantly 3 extravagantly
  4 abundantly

Four sentences – each using one of the words above.

Puzzle corner

A The child's own definitions to the expressions.

  1 e.g. to take the punishment
  2 e.g. to let slip something that should be kept secret
  3 e.g. to face things and get on with it
  4 e.g. to refuse to take sides
  5 e.g. despite disappointment, to get on with things

B Three more expressions the child knows.

Copymaster/Homework answers

Unit 3A

A 1 innocent 2 ignorant 3 different 4 violent
  5 distant 6 silent 7 intelligent 8 important

B 1 abundance 2 chance 3 science 4 residence
  5 instance 6 sentence 7 reference 8 substance

Unit 3B

A 1 merrier 2 leaf 3 dogs 4 bee

B Four sentences, each using an expression found in A.

Suggestions

- Write clues for some of the words covered in this unit. Ask the children to find the *ant* or *ance* words that match the clues.

- There are a few verbs that end with *ant*, e.g. enchant, transplant, disenchant.

- Further extension work can be done highlighting the fact that some adjectives ending in *ant* have related nouns that end in *ancy* e.g. hesitant – hesitancy (vacant, buoyant, expectant, stagnant, etc.).

- Expressions are also covered in Unit 14.

- For a bit of fun ask the children to illustrate the literal meaning of a number of common expressions. Display with their actual meanings written below.

Name: _____   Date: _____

A Add **ent** or **ant** to each of these letters to make a word.

1 innoc_ _ _ _   **2** ignor_ _ _ _

3 differ_ _ _ _   **4** viol_ _ _ _

5 dist_ _ _ _   **6** sil_ _ _ _

7 intellig_ _ _ _   **8** import_ _ _ _

B Add **ence** or **ance** to each of these letters to make a word.

1 abund_ _ _ _ _   **2** ch_ _ _ _ _

3 sci_ _ _ _ _   **4** resid_ _ _ _ _

5 inst_ _ _ _ _   **6** sent_ _ _ _ _

7 refer_ _ _ _ _   **8** subst_ _ _ _ _

If you aren't sure of the endings to any of the words just check them in a dictionary.

Name: _____   Date: _____

Unit 3B

A Complete each of these expressions.

1 The more the _____ .

2 Turn over a new _____ .

3 It's raining cats and _____ .

4 To have a _____ in your bonnet.

B Now use each of the above expressions in a sentence.

1 _____

_____

2 _____

_____

3 _____

_____

4 _____

_____

Unit 4
auto
bi

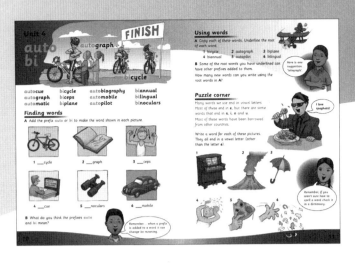

Targets

- to collect and investigate the meanings and spellings of words using the prefixes *auto* and *bi*
- to identify word roots in order to extend vocabulary and provide support for spelling
- to examine the properties of words ending in vowels other than the letter *e*
- to identify everyday words which have been borrowed from other languages, and to understand how this might give clues to spelling

Word list

autocue	bicycle	autobiography	biannual
autograph	biceps	automobile	bilingual
automatic	biplane	autopilot	binoculars

Some other relevant words

autobahn autocracy autocrat automate automation
automotive autonomous autonomy

bicentenary bicolour bifocal bilateral bimonthly
binary binocular bipolar bisect

Relevant high/medium-frequency words

No relevant words.

Pupil Book answers

Finding words

A 1 bicycle 2 autograph 3 biceps 4 autocue
  5 binoculars 6 automobile

B auto means 'self'
  bi means 'two' or 'twice'

Using words

A 1 bicycle 2 autograph 3 biplane 4 biannual
  5 autopilot 6 bilingual

B As many words as the child can make using the roots underlined in **A**, e.g. telegraph, photograph, tricycle, aeroplane

Puzzle corner

1 piano 2 volcano 3 umbrella 4 shampoo
5 pizza 6 confetti

Copymaster/Homework answers

Unit 4A

A Definitions for the following words, with the help of a dictionary.

  1 automatic – a machine that performs a task by itself or with little help
  2 bilingual – able to speak two languages well
  3 autobiography – a piece of writing about the author's own life
  4 biannual – occurring twice a year
  5 autopilot – a machine acting as a pilot (e.g. of a plane)

B Further **auto** or **bi** words found in a dictionary.

Unit 4B

Words associated with music – solo, opera, piano
Words associated with food – spaghetti, pizza, ravioli, pasta, macaroni
(volcano and umbrella circled)

Suggestions

- To introduce these prefixes to the class set a five-minute challenge. Split the class into groups and ask them to record as many words as they can with the *auto* or *bi* prefixes.

- The prefix *auto* means 'self' and the prefix *bi* means 'two' or 'twice'.

- Give the children two sets of cards, one with prefixed words and one with definitions for the prefixed words. Ask the children to match the definitions to the correct words.

- Remind the children that when a prefix is added to a word the root doesn't change.

- Discuss with the children that many words found in our language originated from other languages, either when we were invaded or from countries with which we have had a lot of contact.

- The *Oxford Dictionary of English Etymology* can be used to check the origins of words.

Name: _____   Date: _____

A Use a dictionary to write a definition for each of these words.

1 automatic

_____

2 bilingual

_____

3 autobiography

_____

4 biannual

_____

5 autopilot

_____

B List any more **auto** or **bi** prefixed words you can find in the dictionary.

Name: _____   Date: _____

All these words are 'borrowed' from Italy.
Sort the words into the categories below.

ravioli

solo

pizza

opera

volcano

piano

spaghetti

pasta

macaroni

umbrella

Words associated with music

Words associated with food

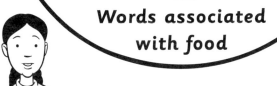

Circle the words that don't fit into either category.

Unit 5
ly

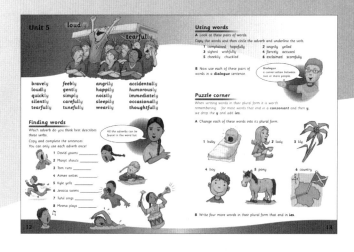

Targets

- to use adverbs to qualify verbs in writing dialogue
- to investigate, collect and classify spelling patterns in pluralisation (+ies), construct rules for regular spellings

Word list

bravely	feebly	angrily	accidentally
loudly	gently	happily	humorously
quickly	simply	noisily	immediately
silently	carefully	sleepily	occasionally
tearfully	tunefully	wearily	thoughtfully

Some other relevant words

beautifully breathlessly correctly cruelly extremely faithfully fiercely fondly fortunately frightfully gratefully haltingly helpfully honestly hopefully insolently interestingly jokingly kindly painfully peacefully playfully pleasantly quietly sadly scornfully successfully usefully vibrantly wonderfully

Relevant high/medium-frequency words

night time

brother different first happy important mother near second world (+ suffix) suddenly

Pupil Book answers

Finding words

Possible adverbs chosen by the child from the word list.

1 sleepily 2 angrily 3 quickly 4 carefully
5 loudly 6 bravely 7 tunefully 8 noisily

Using words

A 1 complained (hopefully) 2 (angrily) yelled

   3 sighed (wishfully) 4 (fiercely) accused

   5 (cheekily) chuckled 6 exclaimed (scornfully)

B Each pair of words in A written in a sentence using dialogue.

Puzzle corner

A 1 babies 2 ladies 3 lilies 4 boys 5 ponies
   6 countries

B Four more words written in their plural form ending in ies.

Copymaster/Homework answers

Unit 5A

1 busily 2 simply 3 heroically 4 cosily
5 joyfully 6 quickly 7 capably 8 tragically
9 funnily 10 carefully

Unit 5B

1 cherries 2 valleys 3 flies 4 Babies 5 days
6 stories 7 activities

Suggestions

- Write on cards questions, statements, exclamations, etc. Ask the children to find appropriate adverb and dialogue words for each card they are given. Encourage them to write the sentences with the adverb and dialogue words, punctuated correctly.

- Ask the children to note dialogue words they find in their reading texts.

- Adverb challenge – In groups, ask the children to find an adverb for every letter of the alphabet.

- Plurals have previously been covered in Book 1, Unit 13; Book 2, Unit 1 and Book 3, Unit 13 and are covered in this book in Units 1 and 7.

- Build a class dictionary of plurals. Each child could be responsible for a page which would illustrate a plural, its singular form, a definition and a picture.

Unit 5A

Here are four rules worth remembering when adding **ly** to words.

- For most words just add **ly** (including words that already end in l).

  cool + ly = coolly

- If a word ends in **y**, then the **y** changes to an **i** before **ly** is added.

  happy + ly = happily

- If a word ends in **ble** or **ple**, then the **le** is dropped and **ly** is added.

  humble + ly = humbly

- If a word ends in **ic**, then usually **ally** is added.

  historic + ly = historically

Add **ly** to each of these words.
Remember the rules above!

1 busy _____   **2** simple _____

3 heroic _____   **4** cosy _____

5 joyful _____   **6** quick _____

7 capable _____   **8** tragic _____

9 funny _____   **10** careful _____

Name: _____   Date: _____

Remember… to make plurals of words that end in a consonant and then **y**, we drop the **y** and add **ies**.

pony    pon**ies**

Choose a word from the box to complete each sentence but change the word you have chosen into its plural form.

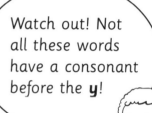
Watch out! Not all these words have a consonant before the **y**!

activity	**valley**	**day**	**fly**
cherry	**baby**	**story**	

1 The _____ tasted delicious.

2 The Welsh _____ are beautiful.

3 The _____ irritated the cows.

4 _____ usually scream when they are tired!

5 It is three _____ until Alice's birthday.

6 Reuben enjoyed listening to the _____ his mum told him.

7 Sarah enjoyed the _____ at summer camp.

Unit 6
tele
trans
circum

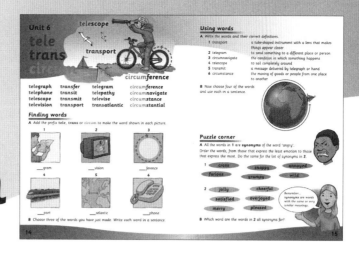

Targets

- to collect and investigate the meanings and spellings of words using the prefixes *tele*, *trans* and *circum*

- to explain the differences between synonyms; collect, classify and order sets of words to identify shades of meaning

Word list

telegraph	transfer	telegram	circumference
telephone	transit	telepathy	circumnavigate
telescope	transmit	televise	circumstance
television	transport	transatlantic	circumstantial

Some other relevant words

telecast telecommunications telephoto lens
teleprinter telesales teletext

circumcise circumfuse circumscribe circumspect
circumvent

Relevant high/medium-frequency words

No relevant words.

Pupil Book answers

Finding words

A **1** telegram   **2** television   **3** circumference
   4 transport   **5** transatlantic   **6** telephone

B Three of the words in **A**, each written in a sentence.

Using words

A **1** transport – the moving of goods or people from one place to another
   2 telegram – a message delivered by telegraph or hand
   3 circumnavigate – to sail completely around
   4 telescope – a tube-shaped instrument with a lens that makes things appear closer
   5 transmit – to send something to a different place or person
   6 circumstance – the condition in which something happens

B Four of the words in **A**, each written in a sentence.

Puzzle corner

A Probable order of words:
   1 snappy, grumpy, annoyed, cross, furious, wild
   2 satisfied, pleased, jolly, cheerful, merry, overjoyed

B These words are all synonyms of the word 'happy'.

Copymaster/Homework answers

Unit 6A

The child's own definitions of the following;

   1 television – electrical equipment that receives sounds and pictures sent over a long distance

   2 transatlantic – anything that moves across the Atlantic ocean

   3 teleprinter – electrical equipment that prints out messages sent from machines in other places

   4 circumnavigate – to navigate around something

   5 transport – the moving of goods through a place or from one place to another

Unit 6B

happy – satisfied, glad, happy, cheerful, delighted

strong – tough, powerful, strong, mighty, invincible

shake – flutter, shiver, shake, vibrate, wobble

Suggestions

- To introduce these prefixes to the class set a five-minute challenge. Split the class into groups and ask them to record as many words as they can with the *circum*, *tele* or *trans* prefixes.

- The prefix *circum* means 'around' or 'about', the prefix *tele* means 'distant' and the prefix *trans* means 'across'.

- Give the children two sets of cards, one with prefixed words and one with definitions for the prefixed words. Ask the children to match the definitions to the correct words.

- Again, remind the children that when a prefix is added to a word the root doesn't change.

- Synonyms have previously been covered in Book 2, Unit 16 and Book 3, Units 6 and 21.

- Look at a previous piece of work the child has written. Discuss how some of the overused words (e.g. some dialogue words, 'got', 'nice', etc.) can be replaced with more interesting synonyms.

- Give the children a set of synonyms with one odd one out. Ask the children to find the odd one out. Ask them to write their own version of the activity and try it out on their friends.

Name: _____   Date: _____

Remember… when prefixes are added to a word they change the meaning of the word in a certain way.

Unit 6A

The table below shows the meanings each prefix can add to a word.

Prefix	Meaning
circum	around
tele	distant, from afar
trans	across, through

Underline the prefix in each of the words below, then write your own definition for each word.

1 television

_____

2 transatlantic

_____

3 teleprinter

_____

4 circumnavigate

_____

5 transport

_____

Check your definitions in a dictionary.

Synonyms are words with the same or very similar meanings.

Complete these synonym ladders.

Order the words, from those that express the **least** at the bottom of the ladder, to those that express the **most** at the top of the ladder.

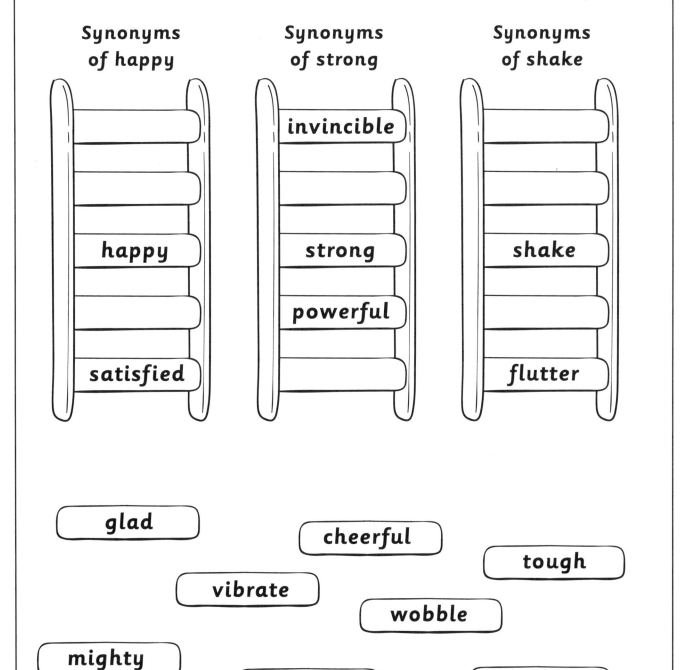

Synonyms of happy: happy, satisfied

Synonyms of strong: invincible, strong, powerful

Synonyms of shake: shake, flutter

glad   cheerful   tough   vibrate   wobble   mighty   shiver   delighted

Unit 7
words to watch

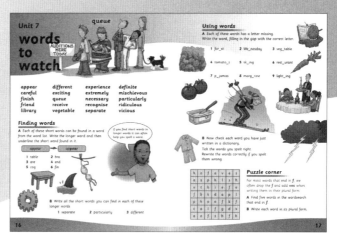

Targets

- to use independent spelling strategies, including: building words from other known words and from awareness of the meaning or derivations of words; using visual skills

- to investigate, collect and classify spelling patterns in pluralisation (+ves), construct rules for regular spellings

Word list

appear	different	experience	definite
careful	exciting	extremely	mischievous
finish	queue	necessary	particularly
friend	receive	recognise	ridiculous
library	vegetable	separate	vicious

Some other relevant words

accidentally agreeable balance character decision
excitement February harass involved jewellery
knowledge leisure medicine occasion opportunity
quarter relevant sincerely temperature twelfth
unnecessary until visitor yacht

Relevant high/medium-frequency words

No relevant words.

Pupil Book answers

Finding words

A 1 vege<u>table</u> 2 <u>library</u> 3 <u>careful</u> 4 <u>friend</u>
5 re<u>cognise</u> 6 de<u>finite</u> or <u>finish</u>

B 1 a, rat, rate, ate, at, (par)
2 particular, part, art, a, (par), (articular)
3 differ, if, rent, (ere), (fer)

Using words

A 1 forest 2 Wednesday 3 vegetable 4 tomatoes
5 skiing 6 restaurant 7 pyjamas 8 margarine
9 lightning

B Words checked by child in dictionary – marked and corrected if need be.

Puzzle corner

A and **B** shelf – shelves calf – calves hoof – hooves
thief – thieves leaf – leaves

Copymaster/Homework answers

Unit 7A

1 across 2 hiccup 3 different 4 carefully
5 traveller 6 offered 7 marriage 8 necessary
9 valleys 10 parallel
Answers marked by child after checking in a dictionary.

Unit 7B

A 1 seven loaves 2 three calves 3 five halves
4 two wolves 5 four thieves 6 nine scarves

B Three sentences, each using the plural form of a word ending in f.

Suggestions

- Use commonly misspelt words in handwriting activities.

- Write the same word on three pieces of paper spelt correctly once. Ask the children to spot the version of the word spelt correctly as quickly as possible.

- Plurals have previously been covered in Book 1, Unit 13; Book 2, Unit 1 and Book 3, Unit 13, and are further covered in this book in Units 1 and 5.

- Build a class dictionary of plurals. Each child could be responsible for a page which would illustrate a plural, its singular form, a definition and a picture.

Name: _____   Date: _____

A One of the letters in each of these words is doubled.
Rewrite each word adding the missing letter.

Like this...   acept   accept

1 acros   _____

2 hicup   _____

3 diferent   _____

4 carefuly   _____

5 traveler   _____

6 ofered   _____

7 mariage   _____

8 necesary   _____

9 valeys   _____

10 paralel   _____

Check and mark your answers
using a dictionary.

Name: _____   Date: _____

A Describe what each picture shows.

Like this...

six leaves

1

_____

2

_____

3

_____

4

_____

5

_____

6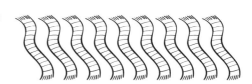

_____

B Write three sentences, each using the plural form of a word ending in f.

1 _____

2 _____

3 _____

Unit 8
silent letters
b g c

Targets

- to use independent spelling strategies including: applying knowledge of spelling rules and exceptions; using visual skills

- to explore onomatopoeia: collect, invent and use words whose meaning is represented in their sounds

Word list

doubt	gnaw	scene	subtle
numbness	gnome	scenic	campaign
plumber	design	scent	foreign
crumb	reign	science	scenery
thumb	sign	scissors	scientist

Some other relevant words

bomber bombshell climber debt dumbfound dumbstruck plumbing subtlety thumbnail thumbscrew

aplomb bomb climb comb dumb limb numb plumb tomb

gnarled gnash gnat diaphragm poignant resign scenario scepter scientific

Relevant high/medium-frequency words

night

light might right

Note – Although these words don't include standard silent letters, it might be useful to highlight these high/medium-frequency words to the children.

Pupil Book answers

Finding words

A plumber thumb gnome sign scissors scientist crumb scent

B Each of the words in **A** with their silent letter circled.

Using words

A

silent b	silent g	silent c
climber	gnarled	scenario
debt	diaphragm	scientific
dumbstruck	gnat	scenery
plumbing	resign	scissors

Two further words added to each column.

B Two sentences, each including words with a **silent b**, **silent g** and **silent c**.

Puzzle corner

Possible answers: **1** a walk in the woods **2** a plughole **3** a pig **4** rain **5** a cat **6** an owl

Copymaster/Homework answers

Unit 8A

A 1 b **2** g **3** g **4** c **5** b **6** g **7** c **8** c **9** b

B wriggle climber knife knocker sword bomb foreign design scent science

Unit 8B

A Possible onomatopoeic words associated with these places:

a train station – whoosh, clunck, click, screech
a beach – crash, giggles, splash, scream
a building site – bang, clang, ouch, thud
a playground – scuffle, skid, scream, slap

B Child's drawing of an animal they have created with associated onomatopoeic words.

Suggestions

- Silent letters have previously been covered in Book 3, Unit 15.

- It is worth highlighting to the children that silent letters are generally consonants; however, some vowel letters aren't always sounded, e.g. head.

- Give the children a list of words with the silent *b*, *c* and *g* left out. Ask them to correct the words adding the missing letters.

- Make a crossword puzzle using words with the silent letters *b*, *c* and *g*. The children could be involved in writing the clues for the words.

- Provide different groups of children with a theme like a fast car, fisherman's boat, etc. Ask the children to write onomatopoeic words to describe associated sounds.

Unit 8A

A Add the missing **silent letters** to these words.

WE WANT MORE POCKET MONEY!

1 clim __

2 __ nat

3 campai __ n

4 mus __ le

5 lam __

6 __ naw

7 s __ ene

8 s __ ientist

9 dou __ t

B Circle the **silent letters** in these words.

wriggle   climber   knife

knocker   sword   bomb

foreign   design   scent   science

These words have the **silent letters b, g** and **c** in them, but also the **silent letters k** and **w**.

Unit 8B

A Write the **onomatopoeic** words
you would associate with these places.

1 a train station _____

2 a beach _____

3 a building site _____

4 a playground _____

B Invent your own onomatopoeic words for an imaginary animal.

Draw your animal and write the words you have invented stating
what they are describing, for example the sound it makes when it eats
or cleans itself.

_____

_____

_____

Unit 9
ful

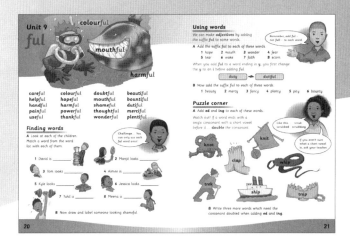

Targets

- to explore spelling patterns of consonants and formulate rules: *ll* in 'full' becomes *l* when used as a suffix

- to explore spelling patterns of consonants and formulate rules: words ending with a single consonant preceded by a short vowel double the consonant before adding *ing* etc.

Word list

careful	colourful	doubtful	beautiful
helpful	hopeful	mouthful	bountiful
handful	harmful	shameful	dutiful
painful	powerful	thoughtful	merciful
useful	thankful	wonderful	plentiful

Some other relevant words

boastful dreadful faithful fearful playful graceful
scornful sorrowful tearful tuneful wakeful

fanciful pitiful

Relevant high/medium-frequency words

help

thought watch (+ suffix)

Pupil Book answers

Finding words

A 1 helpful 2 beautiful 3 thoughtful 4 careful
5 hopeful 6 doubtful 7 powerful 8 thankful

B A labelled picture of someone looking shameful.

Using words

A 1 hopeful 2 mouthful 3 wonderful 4 fearful
5 tearful 6 wakeful 7 faithful 8 scornful

B 1 beautiful 2 merciful 3 fanciful 4 plentiful
5 pitiful 6 bountiful

Puzzle corner

A knotted, knotting   clapped, clapping
knitted, knitting   whipped, whipping
trekked, trekking   shipped, shipping
trapped, trapping

B Three words which need the consonant doubled when adding **ed** and **ing**.

Copymaster/Homework answers

Unit 9A

1 beautiful **2** mouthful **3** fearful **4** plentiful
5 faithful
Five sentences using each of the above words.

Unit 9B

dragged, skipped, signalled, jumped, winked, scrubbed, labelled, packed, hopped

Suggestions

- Highlight to the children that when the word *full* is added to another word an *l* is always dropped.

- With the class, look at the difference between *ful* and *full* when added to the words 'hand' and 'mouth' (*ful* refers to the hand/mouth and *full* refers to the quantity, e.g. 'mouth full of food').

- Challenge the children to find as many roots as they can that have the suffixes *ful* and *ly* both added, e.g. gracefully, scornfully.

- Be sure the children know the difference between long and short vowel sounds.

- Give pairs of children different newspaper articles. Ask them to highlight words where consonants have had to be doubled when a suffix is added.

Unit 9A

Add **ful** to each of these words and then write them in a sentence.

Remember... If a word ends in **y** you need to change the **y** to an **i** before adding **ful**.

1 beauty

_____

_____

2 mouth

_____

_____

3 fear

_____

_____

4 plenty

_____

_____

5 faith

_____

_____

Name: _____   Date: _____

Unit 9B

Look at this picture.
Find as many verbs as you can.

Add **ed** to each verb you have found.

Remember… If a word ends with a single consonant with a short vowel before it, the consonant needs to be doubled.

_____   _____   _____

_____   _____   _____

_____   _____   _____

Unit 10
letter strings

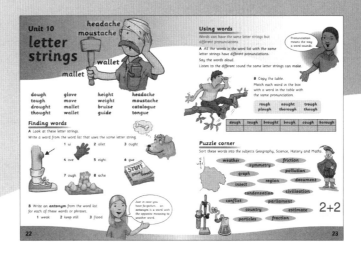

Targets

- to investigate words which have common letter strings but different pronunciations
- to search for, collect, define and spell technical words derived from work in other subjects

Word list

dough	glove	height	headache
tough	move	weight	moustache
drought	mallet	bruise	catalogue
thought	wallet	guide	tongue

Some other relevant words

though plough bough slough cough trough rough
bought fought nought brought sought borough
thorough

love dove grove

eight fight freight light night right sleigh

cruise

bachelor

armour colour could favour four honour hour
journey neighbour route rumour

book boot cook food foot good hood hook hoot
look loot mood nook pool rook root soot took

Relevant high/medium-frequency words

e.g. out your would should could

e.g. thought through brought found around round
sound

Pupil Book answers

Finding words

A 1 bruise or guide 2 mallet or wallet
   3 drought or thought 4 glove or move
   5 weight or height 6 catalogue or tongue
   7 dough or tough 8 headache or moustache

B 1 tough 2 move 3 drought

Using words

A Child to say words aloud.

B

dough	tough	brought	bough	cough	borough
though	rough	nought	plough	trough	thorough

Puzzle corner

History – civilisation parliament document conflict

Geography – pollution region weather country

Maths – estimate graph fraction symmetry

Science – friction particles condensation insect

Copymaster/Homework answers

Unit 10A

The following words circled with the letter string underlined.

1 move 2 flower 3 both 4 echo 5 yellow
6 expensive 7 drought 8 door 9 foot

Unit 10B

The child chooses six words from a subject, then hides them in a wordsearch for a friend to find.

Suggestions

- The children can be given a word group (see 'Some other relevant words'), e.g. *our* or *oo* words. Ask the children to sort the words by sound.

- Pronunciation often depends on preceding and following sounds – possible investigative work can be carried out by the children proving or disproving this.

- Ask the children to compile their own lists of technical words they frequently use.

Name: _____   Date: _____

Unit 10A

Look at these lists of words with the same **letter strings**.

In each list there is an odd one out, where the pronunciation of the letter string is different to the other two words.

Circle the odd one out and underline the letter string.

1	**2**	**3**
move	glow	other
love	flower	brother
glove	blow	both

4	**5**	**6**
echo	clown	expensive
cheese	town	drive
munch	yellow	alive

7	**8**	**9**
sought	door	boot
drought	moon	root
fought	loose	foot

Spelling Book 5 • Unit 10A • letter strings • © *Sarah Lindsay/Atlantic Europe Publishing 2006*

Unit 10B

Choose a subject you enjoy.
Write six words you associate with it.

_____   _____

_____   _____

_____   _____

Like... History (document, revolution), Science (evaporation, apparatus), Maths (subtraction, circumference), ICT (computer, database), etc.

Now create your own wordsearch using these words.
First add the words, then fill the gaps with random letters.

Subject: _____

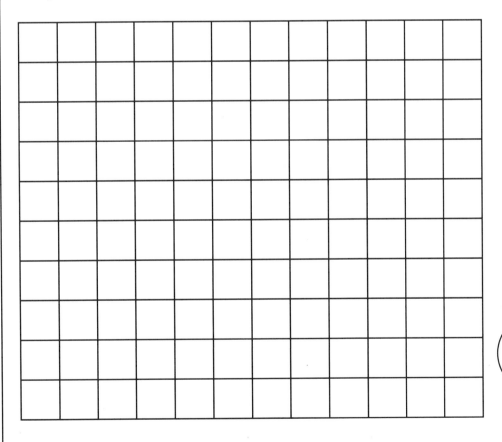

Now try it out on a friend or an adult!

Remember to fold this paper in half or they
will see the words already written at the top of the page!

Unit 11
soft c

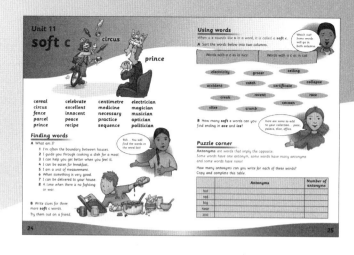

Targets

- to explore spelling patterns of consonants and formulate rules: *c* is usually soft when followed by *i*
- to recognise and spell the suffix *cian*
- to investigate further antonyms

Word list

cereal	celebrate	centimetre	electrician
circus	excellent	medicine	magician
fence	innocent	necessary	musician
parcel	peace	practice	optician
prince	recipe	sequence	politician

Some other relevant words

absence ace acid advance balance bounce
confidence dance December dice entrance fancy
glance grace ice icing juice lace mice mince nice
once pace pence place price race receive replace
resource rhinoceros rice sentence service slice space

ceiling celery cell cement centipede centre century
certain certificate cider cinema circle circuit

beautician dietician paediatrician physician technician

Relevant high/medium-frequency words

once place

Pupil Book answers

Making words

A 1 fence **2** recipe **3** medicine **4** cereal
5 centimetre **6** excellent **7** parcel **8** peace

B The child's own clues for three **soft c** words.

Using words

A Words with a **c** as in nice:
slice, accident, electricity, race, recent, grocer,
certificate, ceiling

Words with a **c** as in cat:
accident, electricity, certificate, collapse, catch,
cocoon, crumb, creak

B Examples of words the child may write:
ace pace palace face lace race space peace
ice dice mice nice rice slice price spice twice

Puzzle corner

	Antonyms (Number of answers may vary)	Number of antonyms
hot	cold chilly cool freezing	e.g. 4
red		0
big	small little tiny narrow slight	e.g. 5
near	far distant	e.g. 2
zoo		0

Copymaster/Homework answers

Unit 11A

A centre sentence currency cinema conspiracy
announce centipede certificate cyclone circular

B A sentence with as many **soft c** words as possible.

Unit 11B

A hot – warm boiling cold steaming
rough – smooth uneven harsh slippery
big – huge tiny small young
arrive – leave exit depart go
happy – cheerful sad upset glum

B Sentences including an antonym of the following
words – secure, scared, miserable, responsible

Suggestions

- If the *c* in a word sounds *s*, it is called a soft *c*.
- Highlight to the children the difference between pract*ice* (noun) and pract*ise* (verb).
- Give the children a number of words with both soft and hard *c*s. Ask them to sort the words according to the sound the *c* makes. Then ask them to sort the words further according to the letter following the *c*. The children should notice that the *ci*, *ce* and *cy* letter combination usually softens the *c*.
- The words Celt and Celtic are exceptions to the *ce* rule (though the football club has a soft *c*).
- Highlight the *cian* suffix and use it to introduce further work on the 'shun' suffixes. See Unit 18 and Book 4, Units 19 and 20.
- Antonyms have previously been covered in Book 2, Unit 8 and Book 3, Unit 11.
- 'Find the opposite' game – Prepare two sets of words, one set of words being the opposite words of the other set (e.g. hot–cold). In pairs the children need to place the cards face down. They take it in turns to turn over two cards aiming to find the two opposite cards. If the cards don't match they need to be turned over again; if they do match that pair of cards belongs to that child. The winner is the one with the most pairs at the end.

Name: _____ Date: _____

A Circle the **soft c** in these words.

conspiracy

currency

announce

circular

centre

cyclone

centipede

sentence

certificate

cinema

B Write a sentence with as many **soft c** words as possible!

You could write a nonsense sentence!

_____

_____

_____

_____

_____

Unit 11B

A Underline the **antonym** or **antonyms** for each word in bold.

hot	warm	boiling	cold	steaming
rough	smooth	uneven	harsh	slippery
big	huge	tiny	small	young
arrive	leave	exit	depart	go
happy	cheerful	sad	upset	glum

B Use an antonym of each of these words in a sentence.

1 secure _____

_____

2 scared _____

_____

3 miserable _____

_____

4 responsible _____

_____

Unit 12
soft g

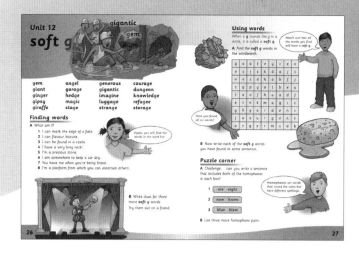

Targets

- to explore spelling patterns of consonants and formulate rules
- to distinguish between homophones, i.e. words with common pronunciations but different spellings

Word list

gem	angel	generous	courage
giant	garage	gigantic	dungeon
ginger	hedge	imagine	knowledge
gipsy	magic	luggage	refugee
giraffe	stage	strange	storage

Some other relevant words

agent biology budget Egyptian engagement fledgling hedgehog imagery imagination legend magician manager margarine margin messenger midget origin original refrigerator regiment region register stranger tragic urgent vegetable

age badge barge cabbage carriage change college damage discourage dodge drainage edge engage enlarge exchange fringe image indulge large ledge manage massage message nudge orange outrage page passage porridge shortage siege wage wedge

general geography germ gin

Relevant high/medium-frequency words

change

Pupil Book answers

Finding words

A **1** hedge **2** ginger **3** dungeon **4** giraffe **5** gem **6** garage **7** courage **8** stage

B The child's own clues for three **soft g** words.

Using words

A Words to be found in wordsearch – sponge cabbage germ urgent magic gentle

B Each of the words found in the wordsearch written in some sentences.

Puzzle corner

A Three sentences, each with one of the following pairs of homophones:
1 ate eight **2** new knew **3** blue blew

B Three more homophone pairs.

Copymaster/Homework answers

Unit 12A

Words with a **soft g** as in **g**iant	Words with a **g** as in **g**oat
register	grocer
package	glossary
stranger	glaze
generous	great
energy	regatta
orange	sugar
angel	wag
margin	gunpowder

Unit 12B

A **1** break **2** which **3** fare **4** course **5** flour **6** you or yew **7** deer **8** quay **9** allowed **10** dough

B Three sentences each with one of the homophones there, their and they're.

Suggestions

- If the *g* in a word sounds *j*, it is called a soft *g*.

- Give the children a number of words with both soft and hard *g*s. Ask them to sort the words according to the sound the *g* makes. Then ask them to sort the words further according to the letter following the *g*. The children should notice that the *gi*, *ge* and *gy* letter combinations usually soften the *g*. However, this rule doesn't work as reliably as for soft *c*.

- Build a class word bank of soft *g* words.

- Give the children a piece of text that includes soft *g* words. Ask the children to underline all the soft *g* words they can find.

- Homophones have previously been covered in Book 4, Units 2 and 20.

- In a given amount of time, challenge the children to write as many homophones as they can think of.

Name: _____   Date: _____

Sort the words into the table.

margin   generous

grocer   **sugar**   angel   glaze

register   **energy**

Words with a **soft g** as in **g**iant	Words with a **g** as in **g**oat

great   wag   **package**

regatta   gunpowder

stranger

orange   **glossary**

Name: _____   Date: _____

Unit 12B

A Next to each word, write a **homophone**.

1 brake _____   **2** witch _____

3 fair _____   **4** coarse _____

5 flower _____   **6** ewe _____

7 dear _____   **8** key _____

9 aloud _____   **10** doe _____

B Write each of the homophones **there**, **their** and **they're** correctly in a sentence.

1 _____

_____

2 _____

_____

3 _____

_____

Unit 13
ure

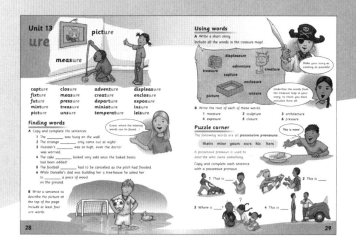

Targets

- to use independent spelling strategies, including building up spellings by syllabic parts, using known suffixes and common letter strings; building words from other known words and from awareness of the meaning or derivations of words; using visual skills

- to identify word roots in order to extend vocabulary and provide support for spelling

- the correct use and spelling of possessive pronouns, linked to work on grammar, e.g. their, theirs; your, yours; my, mine

Word list

capture	closure	adventure	displeasure
fixture	measure	creature	enclosure
future	pressure	departure	exposure
mixture	treasure	miniature	insure
picture	unsure	temperature	leisure

Some other relevant words

acupuncture agriculture aperture architecture
caricature culture curvature denture feature fracture
furniture gesture immature lecture literature
manufacture mature moisture nature nurture pasture
posture premature puncture rapture sculpture
signature structure texture torture venture vulture

assure censure composure disclosure ensure erasure
foreclosure

Relevant high/medium-frequency words

sure

Pupil Book answers

Finding words

A 1 picture 2 creature 3 temperature 4 mixture
   5 fixture 6 measure

B A sentence describing the picture at the beginning of the unit, including at least four **ure** words.

Using words

A A short story including the following words underlined: displeasure adventure treasure capture creature enclosure picture unsure

B 1 moist 2 sculpt 3 architect 4 expose 5 close
   6 press

Puzzle corner

1 his or theirs 2 yours or mine 3 mine
4 ours or mine

Copymaster/Homework answers

Unit 13A

1 fixture 2 sculpture 3 moisture 4 departure
5 pleasure 6 enclosure 7 scripture 8 composure

Unit 13B

A 1 These must be (yours)
   2 I want to wear (mine.)
   3 Have they finished (theirs) yet?
   4 Which one is (ours?)

B Two of the child's own sentences including a possessive pronoun and a picture of each to illustrate.

Suggestions

- There are words in this unit where the *ure* is integral to the actual word, e.g. treasure, and words where the *ure* is added as a suffix, e.g. exposure. Give the children the words in the *Word list* and ask them to distinguish between the different uses of *ure*.

- It is important the children understand that when a suffix is added to a word there is sometimes a need to modify the root word.

- A suffix is a unit of meaning. The suffix *ure* can change the meaning of the word by being a 'state' or 'act of'.

- Do further work on pronouns looking at where they arise in sentences.

- Provide the children with sentences that include possessive pronouns. Ask the children to substitute the pronouns with nouns. Discuss the implications.

Unit 13A

From each of these roots write a word that ends in **sure** or **ture**.

Watch out! Sometimes you will need to change the spelling of the root.

e.g. expose _____exposure_____

1 fix _____

2 sculpt _____

3 moist _____

4 depart _____

5 please _____

6 enclose _____

7 script _____

8 compose _____

DEPARTURES

Name: _____ Date: _____

Remember... A **possessive pronoun** is used to indicate who owns something.

Unit 13B

A Circle the possessive pronoun in each of these sentences.

1 These must be yours.

2 I want to wear mine.

3 Have they finished theirs yet?

4 Which one is ours?

B Now choose two possessive pronouns. Write a sentence using each pronoun and draw a picture to illustrate it.

1 _____

_____

2 _____

_____

Spelling Book 5 • Unit 13B • possessive pronouns • © *Sarah Lindsay/Atlantic Europe Publishing 2006*

Unit 14
al

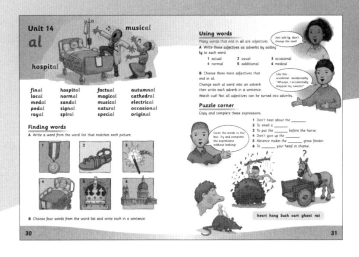

Targets

- to use independent spelling strategies, including building up spellings by syllabic parts, using known prefixes, suffixes and common letter strings; building words from other known words and from awareness of the meaning or derivations of words; using visual skills

- to investigate metaphorical expressions and figures of speech from everyday life

Word list

final	hospital	factual	autumnal
local	normal	magical	cathedral
medal	sandal	musical	electrical
pedal	signal	natural	occasional
royal	spiral	special	original

Some other relevant words

aboriginal accidental actual additional arrival bridal capital casual central clinical comical coral critical dental digital equal general historical horizontal loyal mechanical medical metal moral national petal postal radical removal topical total tropical usual vandal

Relevant high/medium-frequency words

almost also always (al as a prefix)

Pupil Book answers

Finding words

A 1 medal **2** sandal **3** magical **4** hospital **5** royal **6** cathedral

B Four words from the word list, each written in the child's own sentence.

Using words

A 1 actually **2** usually **3** occasionally **4** normally **5** additionally **6** medically

B Three **al** adjectives of the child's choice, each changed into an adverb and then written in sentence.

Puzzle corner

1 Don't beat about the <u>bush</u>. **2** To smell a <u>rat</u>.
3 To put the <u>cart</u> before the horse. **4** Don't give up the <u>ghost</u>. **5** Absence makes the <u>heart</u> grow fonder.
6 To <u>hang</u> your head in shame.

Copymaster/Homework answers

Unit 14A

Noun	Adjective
fact	factual
mechanic	mechanical
origin	original
music	musical
bride	bridal
event	eventual
act	actual
comic	comical
magic	magical
nation	national

Unit 14B

1 When someone is doing a job, but not very carefully.
2 When someone is making a big deal out of a simple job.
3 When someone is assuming something before it has actually happened.
4 To encourage someone to do something now rather than later.

Suggestions

- Discuss with the children that, although *all* is spelt with *ll* when it stands alone, *al* as a suffix or prefix has a single *l*.

- Highlight to the children that the *al* suffix, sounds very similar to both *el* (see Unit 15) and *le* endings.

- It is worth highlighting to the children that some words add *ual* rather than *al*, e.g. actual, eventual.

- Although this unit covers the suffix *al* it might be appropriate to discuss the prefix *al*. It may help the children to know that the spelling of a root word always stays the same when adding a prefix but may change when adding a suffix.

- Find a piece of text where *al* prefixes and suffixes are used. Discuss with the children how it will change the text if the *al* prefixes and suffixes are taken away.

- Expressions are also covered in Unit 3.

- Challenge the children to include some specified expressions in a short story.

- Make a class collection of expressions – can their parents think of any?

Name: _____   Date: _____

Unit 14A

Some nouns can be made into adjectives by adding the **al** suffix.

Fill the gaps in the table by adding the missing nouns or adjectives.

Noun	Adjective
fact	
mechanic	
	original
music	
bride	
	eventual
	actual
comic	
magic	
nation	

Watch out, some of the nouns will change when the suffix is added.

Unit 14B

Explain when these expressions might be used.

1 When a job is worth doing, it's worth doing well.

_____

_____

_____

2 To make a mountain out of a molehill.

_____

_____

_____

3 Don't count your chickens before they're hatched.

_____

_____

_____

4 To strike while the iron is hot.

_____

_____

_____

Unit 15
el

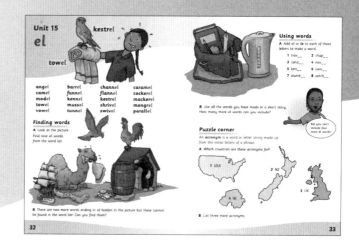

Targets

- to use independent spelling strategies, including building up spellings by syllabic parts, using known prefixes, suffixes and common letter strings; building words from other known words and from awareness of the meaning or derivations of words; using visual skills

- to understand how words can be formed from longer words, through the use of acronyms

Word list

angel	barrel	channel	caramel
camel	funnel	flannel	cockerel
model	kennel	kestrel	mackerel
towel	mussel	shrivel	mongrel
vowel	tunnel	swivel	parallel

Some other relevant words

cancel chapel chisel cruel duffel fuel gravel grovel
hostel hotel hovel level minstrel novel panel parcel
pastel satchel shovel travel vessel

Relevant high/medium-frequency words

No relevant words.

Pupil Book answers

Finding words

A The following words from the word list found in the picture – towel, kestrel, kennel, mongrel, barrel, camel, flannel, cockerel, model.

B Also the following **el** words found in the picture – tinsel, label.

Using words

A 1 travel 2 chapel 3 candle 4 novel 5 kettle
6 swivel 7 stumble 8 satchel

B A short story that includes all of the words from **A** (with a challenge to include more **el** words).

Puzzle corner

A 1 United States of America 2 New Zealand
3 United Kingdom 4 Northern Ireland

B Three more acronyms listed.

Copymaster/Homework answers

Unit 15A
A 1 chapel 2 novel 3 vowel 4 satchel 5 kennel
6 shovel

B Child's own clues for three **el** words.

Unit 15B
A list of the child's own acronyms. Picture prompts for JP, MP, CD, DVD and UK.

Suggestions

- Highlight to the children that the *el* sound is very similar to that of the *al* endings (see Unit 14).

- Make a wordsearch of *el* words for the children to do. Ask them to write a definition for each of the words they have found.

- Explain to the children there are different ways words can be shortened, e.g. abbreviations (DVD), shorter forms of words (maths) and the leaving out of letters (it's).

- Brainstorm as many acronyms as possible. Ask the children to make up a few acronyms of their own.

Name: _____   Date: _____

A Find an **el** word to match each clue.

1 a place of worship   c_____

2 a long story   n_____

3 a type of letter   v_____

4 a type of bag   s_____

5 a dog's house   k_____

6 a type of spade   s_____

B Write your own clues for three **el** words.

1 _____

_____

2 _____

_____

3 _____

_____

Try them out on a friend.

Name: _____   Date: _____

Unit 15B

Make your own list of **acronyms**.

The pictures will help you with some.

 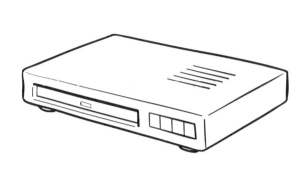 

Acronym	Meaning
CID	Criminal Investigation Department

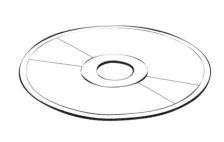 

Unit 16
un
im
il

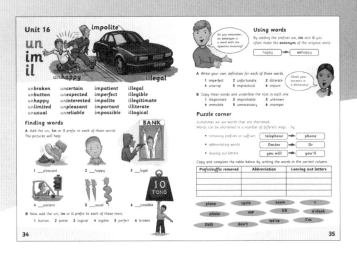

Targets

- to transform words, e.g. negation
- to understand how words can be formed from longer words, e.g. through the omission of letters

Word list

unbroken	uncertain	impatient	illegal
unbutton	unexpected	imperfect	illegible
unhappy	uninterested	impolite	illegitimate
unlimited	unpleasant	important	illiterate
unusual	unreliable	impossible	illogical

Some other relevant words

unable unaccompanied unannounced unapproachable unarmed unattached unaware unbalanced unbearable unborn unchecked unclean uncommon unconscious uncover undecided undo undress uneasy uneaten unemployed unfair unfamiliar unfeeling unfit unfold unfriendly ungrateful unguarded unhealthy unheard unimportant unkind unload unmistakable unnatural unnecessary unpack unreal unreasonable unrest unsuccessful untidy untie untrue unveil unwanted unwell unwilling unwise unwrap unzip

imbalance immaterial immature immeasurable immobile immovable impartial impassive impractical improper impure

Relevant high/medium-frequency words

do just made seen

told sure (+ suffix)

Pupil Book answers

Finding words

A 1 unpleasant **2** unhappy **3** illegal **4** impatient
5 unusual **6** impossible

B 1 unbutton **2** impolite **3** illogical **4** illegible
5 imperfect **6** unbroken

Using words

A The child's own definitions of the following words.

1 imperfect – not perfect
2 unfortunate – to have bad luck
3 illiterate – unable to read and write
4 unwrap – to open
5 impractical – not practical
6 impure – not pure

B 1 illegitimate **2** improbable **3** unknown
4 immobile **5** unnecessary **6** improper

Puzzle corner

Prefix/suffix removed	Abbreviation	Leaving out letters
plane	MP	I'm
cycle	UK	o'clock
exam	v	don't
photo	DVD	we've

Copymaster/Homework answers

Unit 16A

A 1 illegal **2** impatient **3** improbable **4** unlimited
5 illogical **6** immaterial **7** unveil **8** unaware

B The table completed with four prefixed words with **in** and four prefixed words with **dis**.

Unit 16B

hippopotamus Doctor United States of America refrigerator it is is not compact disc mathematics we are perambulator Criminal Investigation Department

Suggestions

- Again, remind the children that when a prefix is added to a word the root doesn't change.

- To introduce these prefixes to the class set a five-minute challenge. Split the class into groups and ask them to record as many words as they can with the *un*, *im* or *il* prefixes.

- The prefixes *un*, *im* and *il* all mean 'not'. The prefix *im* can also mean 'into'.

- Give the children two sets of cards, one with prefixed words and one with definitions for the prefixed words. Ask the children to match the definitions to the correct words.

- Give the children sentences with contracted words. Ask them to write the sentences with the contractions expanded.

Name: _____   Date: _____

A These words have each been given the wrong prefix.
Write the correct spelling next to each word.

1 imlegal   _____

2 unpatient   _____

3 unprobable   _____

4 illimited   _____

5 imlogical   _____

6 inmaterial   _____

7 ilveil   _____

8 ilaware   _____

B The prefixes **in** and **dis** can also make the antonyms of words.
Add four words beginning with each of these prefixes to the table.

in	dis
incorrect	disobey

Name: _____   Date: _____

Unit 16B

Write the longer versions of these shortened words.

Watch out! Some of these are tricky.

hippo _____

Dr _____

USA _____

fridge _____

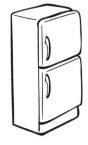

it's _____

isn't _____

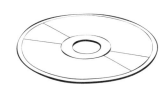

CD _____

maths _____

$$\begin{array}{r} 124- \\ 56 \\ \hline 68 \end{array}$$

we're _____

pram _____

CID _____

Unit 17

er est ish

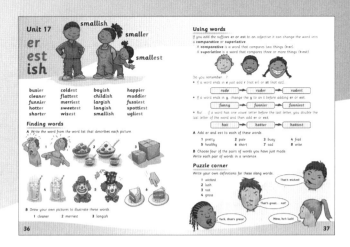

Targets

- to transform words, e.g. making comparatives
- to compile personally written definitions, e.g. of slang, technical terms

Word list

busier	coldest	boyish	happier
cleaner	flattest	childish	muddier
funnier	merriest	largish	fussiest
hotter	sweetest	longish	spottiest
shorter	wisest	smallish	ugliest

Some other relevant words

Comparatives made from the following:

angry black (colour words) big brief calm coarse fierce gloom light lonely lovely slim straight wealthy

Relevant high/medium-frequency words

little new old

happy high light near round small sure white (+ suffix)

Pupil Book answers

Finding words

A **1** hotter **2** sweetest **3** largish **4** coldest **5** funnier **6** smallish

B Child's own pictures illustrating:

1 cleaner **2** merriest **3** longish

Using words

A **1** prettier prettiest **2** paler palest **3** busier busiest **4** frailer frailest **5** healthier healthiest **6** shorter shortest **7** sadder saddest **8** wiser wisest

B Four of the above pairs, each written in a sentence.

Puzzle corner

Child's own definitions of the words:

1 wicked **2** lush **3** not **4** gross

Copymaster/Homework answers

Unit 17A

Child to make comparatives out of given words (with the exception of the words identical, dead and empty) and then include them in sentences.

Unit 17B

The child's choice of eight words associated with Maths. They then write them in alphabetical order with their own definition for each word.

Suggestions

- Comparatives have previously been covered in Book 3, Unit 13.
- Highlight the fact that some words don't have comparatives, e.g. dead, empty. Discuss why. Ask the children to find more.
- It is worth noting to the children that longer adjectives don't have suffixes added but have 'more' or 'most' added.
- Have some fun asking the children to write a made-up word and its definition. Compile a class dictionary of these words with their definitions and, if you like, illustrations.

Unit 17A

Write each of the adjectives
in the box as a **comparative**.

Write each comparative in a sentence.

Watch out!
Three of the
words can't be
written as a
comparative.

| dainty | dead | thin | empty |
| small | brief | lonely | identical |

1 __daintier__

_____

_____

2 _____

_____

_____

3 _____

_____

_____

4 _____

_____

_____

5 _____

_____

_____

Name: _____   Date: _____

Write eight technical words you associate with Maths.

Like... fraction circumference, etc.

Now write your own definition for each word.

Write them in alphabetical order, as found in a dictionary.

Unit 18
ion

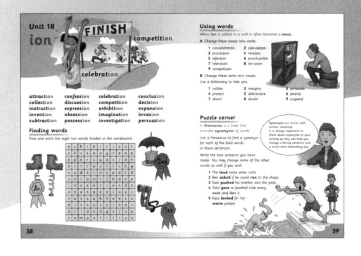

Targets

- to transform words, e.g. verbs to nouns

- to use a thesaurus and understand its purpose

Word list

attraction	confession	celebration	conclusion
collection	discussion	competition	decision
instruction	expression	exhibition	expansion
invention	obsession	imagination	invasion
subtraction	possession	investigation	persuasion

Some other relevant words

admission collision comprehension confusion
conversion depression diversion division erosion
exclusion extension intension intrusion permission
procession progression provision revision suspension
television tension

abbreviation abduction accommodation action
alteration association calculation combination
connection concentration consideration conviction
cooperation correction creation decoration destruction
detection direction dissection distinction donation
education eruption estimation examination expedition
explanation hesitation infection information inspection
invitation irritation objection operation perfection
population prediction prescription protection
punctuation quotation reflection selection separation
vibration

Relevant high/medium-frequency words

No relevant words.

Pupil Book answers

Finding words

invention exhibition competition attraction (traction)
expansion discussion persuasion decision

Using words

A 1 concentrate 2 calculate 3 process 4 revise
   5 infect 6 punctuate 7 televise 8 intrude
   9 compete

B 1 collision 2 imagination 3 persuasion
   4 protection 5 abbreviation 6 extension
   7 diversion 8 division 9 suspension

Puzzle corner

The child is asked to replace words with a synonym
found in a thesaurus.

Copymaster/Homework answers

Unit 18A

A 1 journalism 2 confession 3 suggestion
   4 information 5 baptism 6 insulation
   7 conservation 8 criticism

B Two of the nouns above written in sentences.

Unit 18B

A Three synonyms looked up in a thesaurus for the
following words – 1 feel 2 thin 3 light 4 push
5 love

B Five sentences, each including a synonym of each of
the above words.

Suggestions

- This suffix has previously been covered in Book 4,
  Units 19 and 20.

- It is important the children understand that when a
  suffix is added to a word there is sometimes a need to
  modify the root word.

- A suffix is a unit of meaning. The suffixes *sion*
  and *tion* can change the meaning of the word by
  being an act, a process of or a result of (discussion,
  demolition).

- It is worth highlighting to the children that the
  majority of words with the *shun* sound end in *tion*.
  Also the noun forms of verbs that end in *t*, *te* or *fy*
  usually end in *tion*.

- Thesaurus work has previously been covered in
  Book 3, Unit 7.

- Give the children two sets of cards. The first set of
  words should be synonyms of the words found in
  the second set. Ask the children to match the pairs of
  words as quickly as possible.

Name: _____   Date: _____

As well as the suffix **ion**, the suffix **ism** can also be added
to change **verbs** into **nouns**.

A Choose the correct suffix to change these verbs into nouns.

	ion	ism

1 journal   _____

2 confess   _____

3 suggest   _____

4 inform   _____

5 baptise   _____

6 insulate   _____

7 conserve   _____

8 critic   _____

B Choose two of the words above and write each in a sentence.

1 _____

_____

2 _____

_____

Name: _____   Date: _____

Unit 18B

A Use a **thesaurus**.
Write three **synonyms** for each of these words.

1 feel   _____   _____   _____

2 thin   _____   _____   _____

3 light   _____   _____   _____

4 push   _____   _____   _____

5 love   _____   _____   _____

B Now write a sentence that includes one of the synonyms you have written for each word.

1 feel _____

_____

2 thin _____

_____

3 light _____

_____

4 push _____

_____

5 love _____

_____

Unit 19
en
ify
ise

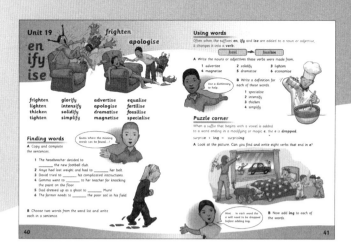

Targets

- to transform words, e.g. nouns (and adjectives) to verbs

- to investigate and learn spelling rules: words ending in modifying *e*, drop *e* when adding *ing*

Word list

frighten	glorify	advertise	equalise
lighten	intensify	apologise	fertilise
thicken	solidify	dramatise	fossilise
tighten	simplify	magnetise	specialise

Some other relevant words

anaesthetise economise terrorise

quicken

Relevant high/medium-frequency words

light (+ suffix)

Pupil Book answers
Finding words

A **1** advertise **2** tighten **3** simplify **4** apologise **5** frighten **6** fertilise

B Two words from the word list, each written in the child's own sentence.

Using words

A **1** advert **2** solid **3** light **4** magnet **5** drama **6** economy

B Child's own definition for the following words:

1 specialise – e.g. to pay special attention to a subject

2 intensify – e.g. to make or become more intense

3 thicken – e.g. to make or become thicker

4 simplify – e.g. to make simple

Puzzle corner

A bite, wake, shake, argue, wave, chase, drive, wipe

B biting, waking, shaking, arguing, waving, chasing, driving, wiping

Copymaster/Homework answers
Unit 19A

1 frighten **2** dramatise **3** specialise **4** solidify
5 lighten **6** apologise **7** glorify **8** fossilise **9** fallen

Unit 19B

A

	+ing	+ed
spray	spraying	sprayed
mime	miming	mimed
invite	inviting	invited
scream	screaming	screamed
squeeze	squeezing	squeezed
consume	consuming	consumed
design	designing	designed
blame	blaming	blamed
stroke	stroking	stroked

B An amusing sentence that includes five of the words the child has made in the table above.

Suggestions

- It is important the children understand that when a suffix is added to a word there is sometimes a need to modify the root word.

- Discuss with the children that they may come across alternative spellings to the *ise* suffix, e.g. *ize*.

- A suffix is a unit of meaning. The suffix *en* can change the meaning of the word by 'becoming' (blacken), *ify* 'to make' (magnify) and *ise* 'to make' or 'to give' (fossilise).

- Adding the suffix *ing* has previously been covered in Book 3, Units 1 and 15.

- Do further extension work looking at words ending in the modifying *e* when a suffix beginning with a consonant or a vowel is added. The *e* is kept rather than dropped with a suffix beginning with a consonant.

- Some useful suffixes beginning with vowels *ing, ed, ish, er, est, ism, able, al*.

- Some useful suffixes beginning with consonants – *ful, ment, less, ness, ly*.

Unit 19A

Add the suffix **en**, **ify** or **ise** to each of these words.

1

_____
(fright)

2

_____
(drama)

3

_____
(special)

4

_____
(solid)

5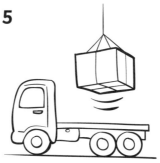

_____
(light)

6

_____
(apology)

7

_____
(glory)

8

_____
(fossil)

9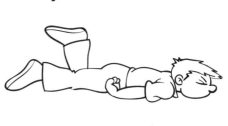

_____
(fall)

Name: _____ Date: _____

A Complete this table.

Remember to drop the modifying **e** when adding a suffix beginning with a vowel.

	+ing	+ed
spray		
mime		
invite		
scream		
squeeze		
consume		
design		
blame		
stroke		

B Use five of the words you have made in one amusing sentence!

_____

_____

_____

_____

_____

Unit 20
tt

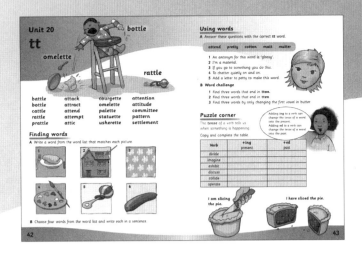

Targets

- to use independent spelling strategies, including: building up spellings by syllabic parts, using known prefixes, suffixes and common letter strings; applying knowledge of spelling rules and exceptions; using visual skills

- to explore spelling patterns of consonants and formulate rules: words ending with a single consonant preceded by a short vowel double the consonant before adding *ing* etc.

- to transform words, e.g. changing tenses

Word list

battle	attack	courgette	attention
bottle	attract	omelette	attitude
cattle	attend	palette	committee
rattle	attempt	statuette	pattern
prattle	attic	usherette	settlement

Some other relevant words

little

batter better bitter butter

button cotton mutton flatten kitten mitten rotten

launderette roulette

chattel guttural latter

matt

Relevant high/medium-frequency words

little

better

Answers

Finding words

A **1** omelette **2** attic **3** pattern **4** palette
5 rattle **6** courgette

B Four words from the word list, each written in the child's own sentences.

Using words

A **1** matt **2** cotton **3** attend **4** mutter **5** pretty

B **1** e.g. cotton button mutton
2 e.g. kitten bitten rotten
3 bitter batter better

Puzzle corner

Verb	+ ing present	+ ed past
divide	dividing	divided
imagine	imagining	imagined
exhibit	exhibiting	exhibited
discuss	discussing	discussed
collide	colliding	collided
operate	operating	operated

Copymaster/Homework answers

Unit 20A

A e.g. rot – rotten, rotting, rotted
bat – batting, batted, batten
gut – gutted, gutting
seat – seated, seating
jot – jotted, jotting, jotter
bet – better, betting, betted
pot – potted, potting, potter

B Child's own amusing sentences using as many words as possible from **A**.

Unit 20B

A Each sentence changed to reflect a different tense.

B Two sentences, one written in the past tense, one in the present tense.

Suggestions

- Double letters have previously been covered in Book 4, Unit 8.

- Highlight to the children how often long vowels in the middle of words are followed by a single consonant while short vowels are often followed by a double consonant.

- Highlight the rules for adding *ing* and *ed* to verbs, e.g. words ending with a single consonant preceded by a short vowel double the consonant before adding *ing*, etc.

- The following letters are never found as 'doubles' in English words – *h, j, k, q, v, w, x.*

- The suffixes *ing* and *ed* have previously been covered in Book 1, Units 16 and 21; Book 2, Units 4 and 6 and Book 3, Units 1 and 15.

- Remind the children that when suffixes are added to a word it can change the root word.

Unit 20A

Remember... when a **suffix** that begins with a vowel is added to words ending in a **short vowel** and **t**, the **t** is doubled.

Watch out! The **t** isn't always doubled!

A Add two or three suffixes to each of these words.

rot			
bat			
gut			
seat			
jot			
bet			
pot			

B Write some amusing sentences that use as many of the words you have made above as possible.

_____

_____

_____

Name: _____   Date: _____

Remember, the **tense** of a verb tells us when something is happening.

Unit 20B

A Write each of these sentences in a different tense.

1 The twins were laughing and screaming as they ran through the sprinkler.

_____

_____

2 Mum is cooking our tea while watching television and talking on the telephone!

_____

_____

3 David's dog limped home after its fight with the dog next door.

_____

_____

4 When Callie was on her way to school she helped an old lady who had slipped on the ice.

_____

_____

B Write two of your own sentences.

One written in the **past** and one in the **present**.

1 _____

2 _____

Unit 21

aw
au

Targets

- to use independent spelling strategies, including building up spellings by syllabic parts, using known prefixes, suffixes and common letter strings; building words from other known words and from awareness of the meaning or derivations of words; using visual skills

- to spell unstressed vowels in polysyllabic words

- to use dictionaries efficiently to explore spellings, meanings (Copymaster 21B)

Word list

crawl	awful	author	applause
prawn	awkward	autograph	audience
straw	drawer	autumn	authority
thaw	sawdust	caught	laundry
yawn	shawl	daughter	thesaurus

Some other relevant words

bawl claw dawn draw drawl drawn fawn flaw hawk jaw law lawn paw pawn raw saw spawn sprawl trawl

audible autocrat autopsy clause haul pause sauce

Relevant high/medium-frequency words

saw because

Pupil Book answers

Finding words

A 1 autumn 2 author 3 straw 4 autograph
5 prawn 6 crawl 7 laundry 8 awful

B The child's own clues for three **aw** or **au** words.

Using words

A 1 applause 2 autograph 3 awkward 4 yawn
5 shawl 6 caught 7 laundry 8 audible
9 sprawl 10 drawl

B Four sentences, each including an **aw** and **au** word.

Puzzle corner

A valuable factory vegetable marmalade history nursery camera

B Three words, each with an unstressed vowel.

Copymaster/Homework answers

Unit 21A

The child creates his/her own wordsearch using nine **aw** and **au** words.

Unit 21B

The following words written correctly and each with a definition:

1 temperature – the measured amount of heat

2 company – a group of people who work together

3 chocolate – a sweet, brown, solid food made from cocoa beans

4 separate – to keep things apart

5 boundary – the edge of an area

6 dictionary – a book where words are listed in alphabetical order with definitions

7 freedom – being free, having no limits

8 jewellery – attractive items to be worn, often made with jewels

Suggestions

- The letter strings *aw* and *au* have previously been covered in Book 2, Unit 15.

- The following letters strings also make the *or* sound in words – *ore* (bore), *oar* (hoarse), *our* (course) and *al* (stalk).

- Using some of the letters strings with the same or similar sound, encourage the children to find homophones with the *au* or *aw* letter strings, e.g. court/caught, roar/raw.

- Unstressed vowels can be a hard concept for children to grasp. Owing to dialect variations it isn't always easy to be exact about stressed and unstressed vowels in words.

- Ask the children to find examples of unstressed vowels in their own work to add to a class word bank. Look for patterns in the words they have found.

- Have fun creating mnemonics for words with unstressed vowels.

- Remind the children about all the information a dictionary can provide (e.g. information about words, their origins and multiple meanings) and that this can provide a guide to spelling.

- Ask the children to find an interesting word in a dictionary and present that word to the rest of the group/class detailing all the information about it. Does it have an unstressed vowel?

Unit 21A

Write nine **aw** or **au** words.

The letter patterns can be at the beginning or in the middle of a word.

Use a dictionary to help if you run out of ideas!

Now make your own wordsearch using these words.

Here is how you do it!
Use a pencil in case you need to change something.
First write your nine words in the grid on the right, then fill the spaces with any other letters.
Make sure you spell the words correctly or they will be impossible to find!

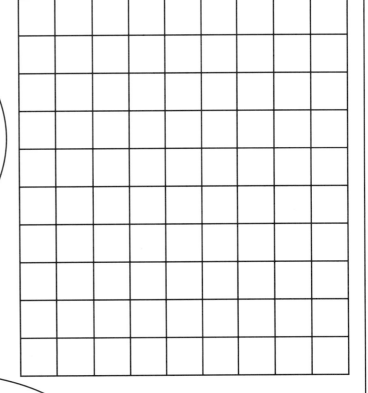

Now try it out on a friend or an adult!
Remember to fold this paper in half or they will see the words already written at the top of the page!

Name: _____   Date: _____

Unit 21B

Each of the words below has an **unstressed vowel** missing.

Write the correct spelling and
a definition for each word.

Use a dictionary
to help.

1 temprature

_____   _____

2 compny

_____   _____

3 choclate

_____   _____

4 seprate

_____   _____

5 boundry

_____   _____

6 dictionry

_____   _____

7 freedm

_____   _____

8 jewellry

_____   _____

Spelling Book 5 • Unit 21B • unstressed vowels • © *Sarah Lindsay/Atlantic Europe Publishing 2006*

Unit 22
ph

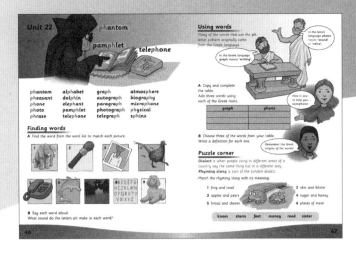

Targets

- to use independent spelling strategies, including building up spellings by syllabic parts, using known prefixes, suffixes and common letter strings; building words from other known words and from awareness of the meaning or derivations of words; using visual skills

- to understand how words vary across dialects

Word list

phantom	alphabet	graph	atmosphere
pheasant	dolphin	autograph	biography
phone	elephant	paragraph	microphone
photo	pamphlet	photograph	physical
phrase	telephone	telegraph	sphinx

Some other relevant words

calligraphy claustrophobia euphoria geography graph graphic hemisphere hyphen metaphor orphan pharmacy pharmaceutical phase phonic phonological phosphorous photography physics physicist physiotherapy prophet saxophone sphere sphinx symphony

Relevant high/medium-frequency words

No relevant words.

Pupil Book answers

Finding words

A 1 elephant 2 microphone 3 photograph or photo
4 pheasant 5 telephone or phone 6 dolphin
7 phantom 8 alphabet 9 sphinx

B The letters **ph** make the sound ∫.

Using words

A Examples of words the children could include in their table.

graph	phone
photograph	telephone
telegraph	microphone
autograph	saxophone

B The child's own definitions for three of the words written in the table.

Puzzle corner

1 frog and toad – road
2 skin and blister – sister
3 apples and pears – stairs
4 sugar and honey – money
5 bread and cheese – knees
6 plates of meat – feet

Copymaster/Homework answers

Unit 22A

1 (correct) 2 pamphlet 3 dolphin 4 (correct)
5 phone 6 saxophone 7 orphan 8 pharmacy
9 (correct) 10 alphabet

Unit 22B

banger – old car   aye – yes   nipper – small boy
scarper – run away   wee – little   scoff – eat
tatties – potatoes   daps – plimsolls

Suggestions

- Most *ph* words are Greek in origin – highlight the fact that some of the words we use are borrowed from other languages and that some words evolve.

- Research for further words can be done in some dictionaries.

- Give the children a number of *ph* words and ask them to write, then check, their definitions.

- The children will enjoy making up their own rhyming slang for given words.

- Read aloud poems that use dialect, e.g. poems by John Agard.

- Discuss dialects found in different British soaps, e.g. *Coronation Street* and *EastEnders*.

Unit 22A

Mike has completed a spelling test.

Unfortunately he has made the same mistake in many of the words.

Instead of writing **ph** for the **f** sound he has written an **f.**

Mark Mike's spelling test. Write the correct spelling next to all the words he has spelt incorrectly, but watch out... some of the words do need an **f**!!

1 flash ☐ _____

2 pamflet ☐ _____

3 dolfin ☐ _____

4 knife ☐ _____

5 fone ☐ _____

6 saxofone ☐ _____

7 orfan ☐ _____

8 farmacy ☐ _____

9 function ☐ _____

10 alfabet ☐ _____

Name: _____   Date: _____

Join the **dialect words** with their meanings.

 old car    little   eat    potatoes

banger   aye   nipper

scarper

wee

scoff   daps

tatties

 run away    small boy    yes    plimsolls

Pupil Assessments

Assessment notes and answers

Book 5 Pupil Assessment A

Book 5 Pupil Assessment B

Assessment notes and answers

Notes

- There are two assessments: Pupil Assessment A covering units 1–11 and Pupil Assessment B covering units 12–22 from the *Pupil Book*.

- Each question represents the spelling focus of a unit.

- The questions the pupil struggles with represent the spelling focus the child needs further work on.

- It is suggested the child does the assessment in a relatively quiet environment.

- Ensure the pupils can read the questions before commencing the Assessment activity.

Answers

Pupil Assessment A

1   choir cheese
2   fence present sentence
3   appearance instant or instance glance entrant or entrance balance giant
4   Two words with the prefix **auto** and two with the prefix **bi**.
5   Adverbs that reflect the verbs screamed, sung and marched
6   transatlantic telescope circumference circumstance
7   vegetable library necessary different
8   design scissors thumb plumber scent foreign
9   fearful beautiful powerful plentiful
10 A word with the same letter string but different pronunciation to cough, love, four and cow.
11 The following words circled – certificate peace recipe cinema.

Pupil Assessment B

1   The following words circled – strange giant ribcage garage siege
2   treasure temperature exposure measure adventure picture
3   Three words that end in **al**.
4   The following words ticked – mackerel camel kennel
5   impolite unpleasant illogical impatient
6   smallish funniest ruder hottest
7   protection division instruction invasion
8   solidify thicken quicken apologise intensify
9   attempt attract statuette attention
10 autumn shawl laundry yawn awkward author
11 Four words that include the **ph** letter string.

Name: _____   Date: _____

1 Solve the clues to find the **ch** words.

A group of singers.   _____

You can eat this with pickle.   _____

2 Add **ent** or **ence** to complete each word.

      Add **ent** or **ence** to complete each word.

f_____   pres_____   sent_____

3 Add **ant** or **ance** to make a word.

appear_____   inst_____   gl_____

entr_____   bal_____   gi_____

4 Write two words with the prefix **auto** and two words with the prefix **bi**.

_____ _____ _____ _____

5 Write an adverb to go with each of these verbs.

screamed_____   sung_____   marched_____

6 Add the **tele**, **trans** or **circum** prefix to each of these words.

_____atlantic   _____scope

_____ference   _____stance

Name: _____   Date: _____

7 Each of these words has a letter missing.
Spell each of the words correctly.

vegtable _____   libary _____

necesary _____   diffrent _____

8 Circle the **silent letter** in each of these words.

design   **scissors**   **thumb**

plumber   **scent**   **foreign**

9 Add the suffix **ful** to each of these roots.

fear _____   beauty _____

power _____   plenty _____

10 Write a word with the same letter string but that has a different pronunciation.

cough _____   love _____

four _____   cow _____

11 Circle the words with a **soft c**.

certificate   **cake**   **peace**

recipe   **cinema**   **cathedral**

Name: _____   Date: _____

1 Circle the words with a **soft g**.

strange   giant   ribcage   goat

garage   underground   siege

2 Add **sure** or **ture** to make a word.

trea_____   tempera_____   expo_____

mea_____   adven_____   pic_____

3 Write three words that end in **al**.

_____   _____   _____

4 Tick the words that are spelt correctly.

shrival ☐   mackerel ☐   camel ☐

barral ☐   kennel ☐

5 Add the **un**, **im** or **il** prefix to each of these roots.

____polite   ____pleasant   ____logical   ____patient

6 Complete these word sums.

small + ish = _____   funny + est = _____

rude + er = _____   hot + est = _____

Name: _____ Date: _____

7 Change these words from verbs to nouns by adding the suffix **ion**.

protect _____   divide _____

instruct _____   invade _____

8 Add the **en**, **ify** or **ise** suffix to each of these roots.

solid   _____   thick   _____

quick   _____   apology _____

intense _____

9 Each of these words has a double **t** missing.
Rewrite each word correctly.

atempt _____   atract _____

statuete _____   atention _____

10 Add **aw** or **au** to make a word.

__ __tumn   sh__ __l   l__ __ndry   y__ __n   __ __kward   __ __thor

11 Write four words that include the **ph** letter string.

_____   _____

_____   _____

Look Cover Say Write Check

Unit word lists

Medium-frequency (MF) word lists

Look Cover Say Write Check copymaster

Look Cover Say Write Check

Unit word lists

The following lists of words from each unit are designed to be photocopied. If required they can be stuck to the photocopiable sheet on page 96 and used as the spelling homework for the week. The words can be split according to the ability of the child, e.g. one child might take home all twenty spellings while another may take just ten.

Medium-frequency words

It is important that the children are very familiar with the medium-frequency words. It is crucial they learn to spell them as soon as they are able. As well as having various exercises throughout the scheme we have also included them as lists of spelling/homework words. The words have been listed in groups of six, as logically as possible.

High-frequency words can be found in the same format in *Teacher's Resource Books* 1 to 3.

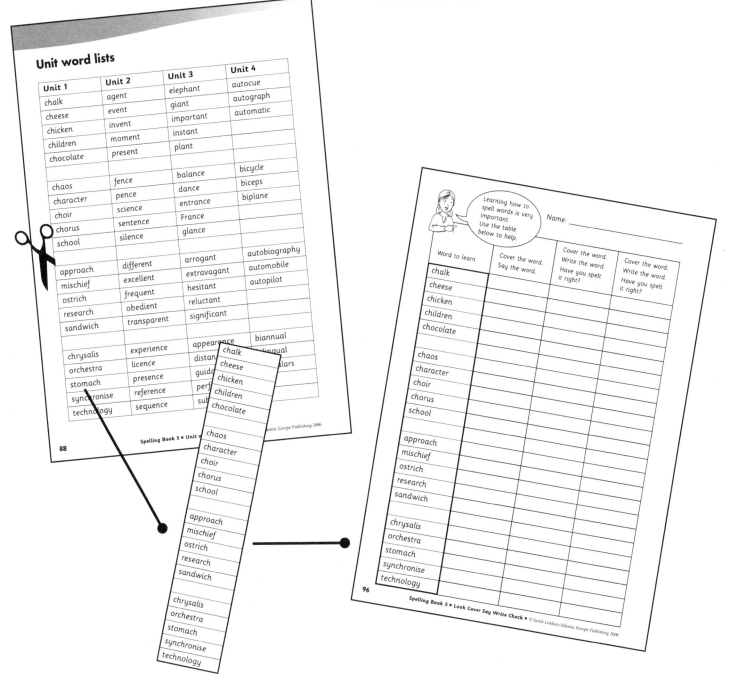

Unit word lists

Unit 1	Unit 2	Unit 3	Unit 4
chalk	agent	elephant	autocue
cheese	event	giant	autograph
chicken	invent	important	automatic
children	moment	instant	
chocolate	present	plant	
chaos	fence	balance	bicycle
character	pence	dance	biceps
choir	science	entrance	biplane
chorus	sentence	France	
school	silence	glance	
approach	different	arrogant	autobiography
mischief	excellent	extravagant	automobile
ostrich	frequent	hesitant	autopilot
research	obedient	reluctant	
sandwich	transparent	significant	
chrysalis	experience	appearance	biannual
orchestra	licence	distan	...lingual
stomach	presence	guid	...lars
synchronise	reference	perf	
technology	sequence	sub	

88   Spelling Book 5 • Unit ...   ...antic Europe Publishing 2006

Cut-out strip:
chalk / cheese / chicken / children / chocolate / chaos / character / choir / chorus / school / approach / mischief / ostrich / research / sandwich / chrysalis / orchestra / stomach / synchronise / technology

Worksheet (page 96):

Learning how to spell words is very important. Use the table below to help.

Name: _____

Word to learn	Cover the word. Say the word.	Cover the word. Write the word. Have you spelt it right?	Cover the word. Write the word. Have you spelt it right?
chalk			
cheese			
chicken			
children			
chocolate			
chaos			
character			
choir			
chorus			
school			
approach			
mischief			
ostrich			
research			
sandwich			
chrysalis			
orchestra			
stomach			
synchronise			
technology			

96   Spelling Book 5 • Look Cover Say Write Check • © Sarah Lindsay/Atlantic Europe Publishing 2006

Unit word lists

Unit 1	Unit 2	Unit 3	Unit 4
chalk	agent	elephant	autocue
cheese	event	giant	autograph
chicken	invent	important	automatic
children	moment	instant	
chocolate	present	plant	
chaos	fence	balance	bicycle
character	pence	dance	biceps
choir	science	entrance	biplane
chorus	sentence	France	
school	silence	glance	
approach	different	arrogant	autobiography
mischief	excellent	extravagant	automobile
ostrich	frequent	hesitant	autopilot
research	obedient	reluctant	
sandwich	transparent	significant	
chrysalis	experience	appearance	biannual
orchestra	licence	distance	bilingual
stomach	presence	guidance	binoculars
synchronise	reference	performance	
technology	sequence	substance	

Unit word lists

Unit 5	Unit 6	Unit 7	Unit 8
bravely	telegraph	appear	doubt
loudly	telephone	careful	numbness
quickly	telescope	finish	plumber
silently	television	friend	crumb
tearfully		library	thumb
feebly	transfer	different	gnaw
gently	transit	exciting	gnome
simply	transmit	queue	design
carefully	transport	receive	reign
tunefully		vegetable	sign
angrily	telegram	experience	scene
happily	telepathy	extremely	scenic
noisily	televise	necessary	scent
sleepily	transatlantic	recognise	science
wearily		separate	scissors
accidentally	circumference	definite	subtle
humorously	circumnavigate	mischievous	campaign
immediately	circumstance	particularly	foreign
occasionally	circumstantial	ridiculous	scenery
thoughtfully		vicious	scientist

Unit word lists

Unit 9	Unit 10	Unit 11	Unit 12
careful	dough	cereal	gem
helpful	tough	circus	giant
handful	drought	fence	ginger
painful	thought	parcel	gipsy
useful		prince	giraffe
colourful	glove	celebrate	angel
hopeful	move	excellent	garage
harmful	mallet	innocent	hedge
powerful	wallet	peace	magic
thankful		recipe	stage
doubtful	height	centimetre	generous
mouthful	weight	medicine	gigantic
shameful	bruise	necessary	imagine
thoughtful	guide	practice	luggage
wonderful		sequence	strange
beautiful	headache	electrician	courage
bountiful	moustache	magician	dungeon
dutiful	catalogue	musician	knowledge
merciful	tongue	optician	refugee
plentiful		politician	storage

Unit word lists

Unit 13	Unit 14	Unit 15	Unit 16
capture	final	angel	unbroken
fixture	local	camel	unbutton
future	medal	model	unhappy
mixture	pedal	towel	unlimited
picture	royal	vowel	unusual
closure	hospital	barrel	uncertain
measure	normal	funnel	unexpected
pressure	sandal	kennel	uninterested
treasure	signal	mussel	unpleasant
unsure	spiral	tunnel	unreliable
adventure	factual	channel	impatient
creature	magical	flannel	imperfect
departure	musical	kestrel	impolite
miniature	natural	shrivel	important
temperature	special	swivel	impossible
displeasure	autumnal	caramel	illegal
enclosure	cathedral	cockerel	illegible
exposure	electrical	mackerel	illegitimate
insure	occasional	mongrel	illiterate
leisure	original	parallel	illogical

Unit word lists

Unit 17	Unit 18	Unit 19	Unit 20
busier	attraction	frighten	battle
cleaner	collection	lighten	bottle
funnier	instruction	thicken	cattle
hotter	invention	tighten	rattle
shorter	subtraction		prattle
coldest	confession	glorify	attack
flattest	discussion	intensify	attract
merriest	expression	solidify	attend
sweetest	obsession	simplify	attempt
wisest	possession		attic
boyish	celebration	advertise	courgette
childish	competition	apologise	omelette
largish	exhibition	dramatise	palette
longish	imagination	magnetise	statuette
smallish	investigation		usherette
happier	conclusion	equalise	attention
muddier	decision	fertilise	attitude
fussiest	expansion	fossilise	committee
spottiest	invasion	specialise	pattern
ugliest	persuasion		settlement

Unit word lists

Unit 21	Unit 22
crawl	phantom
prawn	pheasant
straw	phone
thaw	photo
yawn	phrase
awful	alphabet
awkward	dolphin
drawer	elephant
sawdust	pamphlet
shawl	telephone
author	graph
autograph	autograph
autumn	paragraph
caught	photograph
daughter	telegraph
applause	atmosphere
audience	biography
authority	microphone
laundry	physical
thesaurus	sphinx

Medium-frequency (MF) word lists

MF Words 1	MF Words 4	MF Words 7	MF Words 10
asked	coming	almost	any
jumped	walking	always	better
opened	stopped	every	morning
started	used	never	still
turned	tries	only	upon
walked	woken	suddenly	young

MF Words 2	MF Words 5	MF Words 8	MF Words 11
began	knew	first	above
being	know	second	across
brought	change	last	along
thought	think	half	around
found	leave	today	between
heard	should	year	inside

MF Words 3	MF Words 6	MF Words 9	MF Words 12
I'm	gone	before	below
can't	told	during	following
didn't	show	sometimes	high
don't	much	often	near
does	watch	until	through
goes	write	while	under

Medium-frequency (MF) word lists

MF Words 13	MF Words 15	MF Words 17	MF Words 19
also	baby	great	white
both	happy	sure	light
different	children	those	why
round	garden	word	eyes
such	head	work	window
without	heard	world	own

MF Words 14	MF Words 16	MF Words 18	MF Words 20
other	balloon	father	earth
outside	birthday	mother	important
place	brother	lady	money
right	clothes	sister	small
together	something	paper	sound
where	swimming	friends	whole

Learning how to spell words is very important.
Use the table below to help.

Name: _____

Word to learn	Cover the word. Say the word.	Cover the word. Write the word. Have you spelt it right?	Cover the word. Write the word. Have you spelt it right?

Spelling Book 5 • Look Cover Say Write Check • © *Sarah Lindsay/Atlantic Europe Publishing 2006*